Visual Factfinder

PLANET EARTH

Visual Factfinder

PLANET EARTH

NEIL CURTIS AND MICHAEL ALLABY

Kingfisher Books

NEW YORK

KINGFISHER BOOKS
Grisewood & Dempsey Inc.
95 Madison Avenue
New York, New York 10016

First American edition 1993
2 4 6 8 10 9 7 5 3 1 (lib. bdg.)
2 4 6 8 10 9 7 5 3 1 (pbk.)

Library of Congress Cataloging-in-Publication Data
Curtis, Neil.
Planet earth/Neil Curtis.—1st American ed.
p. cm.—(Visual factfinders)
Includes index.
Summary: Text and illustrations, diagrams, tables, and charts
present information on such topics as surface features of Earth,
weather and climate, natural resources, and environmental problems.
1. Earth—Juvenile literature. [1. Earth.] I. Title,
II. Series.
QB631.4.M85 1993
550—dc20   93-20103 CIP AC

ISBN 1-85697-848-6 (lib. bdg.)
ISBN 1-85697-847-8 (pbk.)

Series Editor: Michèle Byam
Editor: Andrea Moran
Series Designer: Ralph Pitchford
Designer: Nigel Bradley
Picture Research: Su Alexander and Elaine Willis

Additional help from Nicky Barber, Catherine Headlam, Andy Archer, Julian Ewart,
Matthew Gore, Mustafa Sidki, Martin Wilson, Janet Woronkowicz, Hilary Bird

Printed in Spain

CONTENTS

About this Factfinder

Through the dynamic combination of words and pictures, this encyclopedic reference book presents a wealth of facts and figures in an instantly accessible form. It describes the Earth's structure, its diverse landforms, its oceans and atmosphere, and includes such topics as natural resources and the environment.

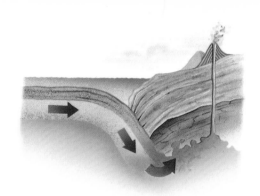

Short text essays introduce each of the Earth's key features, including more specialized topics such as volcanoes, and winds and storms.

Captions provide detailed information, explaining diagrams and highlighting examples of different rocks, minerals, rivers, lakes, clouds, and storms.

Photographs and satellite images provide a further source of visual information on areas such as the oceans, atmosphere, weather, erosion, and resources.

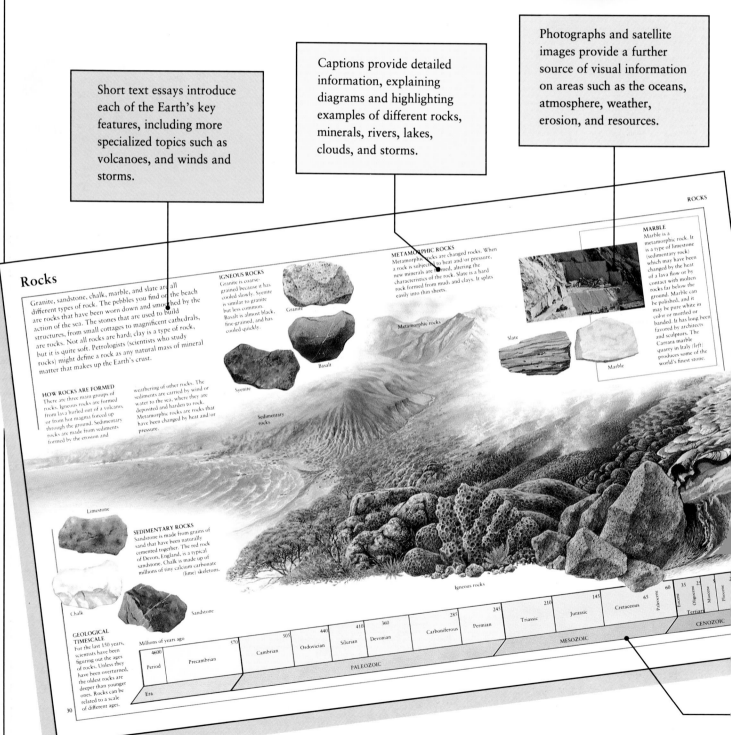

ROCKS

Rocks

Granite, sandstone, chalk, marble, and slate are all different types of rock. The pebbles you find on the beach are rocks that have been worn down and smoothed by the action of the sea. The stones that are used to build structures, from small cottages to magnificent cathedrals, are rocks. Not all rocks are hard; clay is a type of rock, but it is quite soft. Petrologists (scientists who study rocks) might define a rock as any natural mass of mineral matter that makes up the Earth's crust.

HOW ROCKS ARE FORMED
There are three main groups of rocks. Igneous rocks are formed from lava hurled out of a volcano, or from hot magma forced up through the ground. Sedimentary rocks are made from sediments formed by the erosion and weathering of other rocks. The sediments are carried by wind or water to the sea, where they are deposited and harden to rock. Metamorphic rocks are rocks that have been changed by heat and/or pressure.

IGNEOUS ROCKS
Granite is coarse-grained because it has cooled slowly. Syenite is similar to granite but less common. Basalt is almost black, fine-grained, and has cooled quickly.

Granite

Basalt

Syenite

METAMORPHIC ROCKS
Metamorphic rocks are changed rocks. When a rock is subjected to heat and/or pressure, new minerals are formed, altering the characteristics of the rock. Slate is a hard rock formed from mud, and clays. It splits easily into thin sheets.

Metamorphic rocks

Slate

MARBLE
Marble is a metamorphic rock. It is a type of limestone (sedimentary rock) which may have been changed by the heat of a lava flow or by contact with molten rocks far below the ground. Marble can be polished, and it may be pure white in color or mottled or banded. It has long been favored by architects and sculptors. The Carrara marble quarry in Italy (left) produces some of the world's finest stone.

Marble

Sedimentary rocks

Limestone

SEDIMENTARY ROCKS
Sandstone is made from grains of sand that have been naturally cemented together. The red rock of Devon, England, is a typical sandstone. Chalk is made up of millions of tiny calcium carbonate (lime) skeletons.

Chalk

Sandstone

Igneous rocks

GEOLOGICAL TIMESCALE
For the last 150 years, scientists have been figuring out the ages of rocks. Unless they have been overturned, the oldest rocks are deeper than younger ones. Rocks can be related to a scale of different ages.

Millions of years ago	4600	570	505	440	410	360	285	245	210	145	65	60	35	22		
Period	Precambrian	Cambrian	Ordovician	Silurian	Devonian	Carboniferous	Permian	Triassic	Jurassic	Cretaceous	Paleocene	Eocene	Oligocene	Miocene	Pliocene	
Era			PALEOZOIC						MESOZOIC				CENOZOIC	Tertiary		

30

Polar Regions and the Tundra

Within the Arctic and Antarctic circles there is at least one day a year when the Sun does not rise, and at least one when it does not set. The Arctic and Antarctic are lands of midnight Sun in summer, and noon darkness in winter. The polar regions are the coldest on Earth, and among the driest because there is little liquid water. Most of Greenland lies beneath ice 5,000 ft. (1,500 m) thick, that fills valleys and buries hills. The average thickness of the Antarctic ice sheet is more than 6,500 ft. (2,000 m).

THE ARCTIC AND THE ANTARCTIC

Most of Greenland and the northern parts of Alaska, Canada, Scandinavia, and Siberia lie within the Arctic Circle, but there is no land close to the North Pole itself. Antarctica is the world's fifth largest continent, divided into two parts by the Transantarctic Mountains. Beneath the ice, the land of East Antarctica is mostly rugged, in places rising to more than 13,000 ft. (4,000 m) above sea level. West Antarctica is lower. Much of it is made up of a peninsula and island archipelago. In places, the land around the South Pole is up to 8,200 ft. (2,500 m) below sea level.

THE TUNDRA

Around the Arctic Circle, between the conifer forests farther south and the region of permanent ice to the north, the tundra extends as a vast treeless plain across all the northern continents. In summer the ground thaws for just a few weeks, triggering frantic activity for the region's animals and plants.

ICEBERGS

An iceberg is a large block of floating ice. It looks much larger than it looks because some nine-tenths of the ice floats below the surface. This can be dangerous to ships. Some Antarctic icebergs are more than 60 mi. (100 km) long.

Sea level

Glacier or ice sheet

Tundra

Ice cap

Greater Antarctica

Transantarctic mountains

Height (miles)
1.25
0.5
0.5
-0.5

600 miles

1,250 miles

Ice sheet

Ross Ice Shelf

Lesser Antarctica

Ice sheet

2,000 miles

2,500 miles

3,000 miles

▼ Where a glacier enters the sea, the ice floats on the water. The end of the glacier snaps off to form an iceberg. Ice shelfs also break, forming much larger icebergs.

▼ Under the Antarctic ice sheet, unlike the Arctic, there is land. Near the coasts some glaciers have retreated, leaving dry, rocky valleys, called "oases." Inland, high mountain peaks project above the ice, as "nunataks."

▼ Geese, waders, and sea birds live on the tundra. Tundra mammals include polar and grizzly bears, musk ox, caribou, voles, and shrews.

Pingo

Dwarf birch

Lichen

▼ Tundra plants are small, as their roots can only grow to a depth of 12 in. (30 cm) before they reach frozen ground. There are heaths, dwarf birch trees, sedges and rushes, mosses and lichens. Many plants flower in the brief summer.

FACTS ABOUT POLAR LANDS

- During the dark nights, plant nutrients accumulate in the sea. As the light returns, marine plants multiply rapidly, providing food for small and larger animals, such as fish, sea birds, seals, and whales.
- Each year, more than 7,000 icebergs are carried south from Greenland in the Labrador Current.

Pack ice
Drift ice
Ice shelves
Ice sheet
Tree line

North Pole

South Pole

Greenland

ANTARCTIC

ARCTIC

▲ The extent of the Antarctic ice sheet varies with the changing seasons. In winter the drift ice extends out to the southern tip of South America. The Antarctic is home to a few plants and some insects. In summer, penguins, sea birds, and seals visit it.

▲ The Arctic is a mass of pack ice which also changes with the seasons. In winter, its ice covers all of Greenland and its drift ice reaches as far south as Iceland and northern Russia. The presence of the ice and tundra lands limits the growth of trees to areas south of the line through northern Canada, Norway, Sweden, and Russia.

PERMAFROST

In winter, in the Arctic and Antarctic, all the moisture in the soil freezes, but in some areas the top few inches of the soil thaw in summer. During the summer thaw, the ground turns to mud, with pools in the hollows. The subsoil and deeper layers remain permanently frozen. They are called "permafrost." If the permafrost thaws, for example, because of the heating effect of a house or oil pipeline, then the land will sink.

Soil thaws in summer

Permafrost

POLAR RESOURCES

Long ago, the polar regions lay in lower latitudes and had warmer climates. In Antarctica, there are deposits of coal up to 20 ft. (6 m) thick, formed 250 million years ago. Alaska also has vast coal reserves, and, in 1968, one of the world's largest oil fields was discovered at Prudhoe Bay.

▼ Oil travels south from Alaska to ports by the Trans-Alaska Pipeline. The pipeline was built on supports above the ground, to prevent it thawing the permafrost.

65

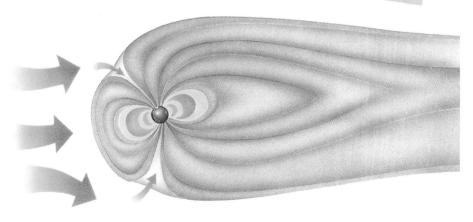

8 *This landscape on the island of Sardinia, Italy, shows one of the many pressures that have shaped the Earth's surface.*

PLANET EARTH

Only in the last decade or two have we been able to appreciate our world in all its splendor —since satellites have sent back photographs of our watery globe. Without such pictures it is hard to imagine that Earth is a ball-shaped planet traveling around the Sun through the vastness of space.

But scientists and great thinkers have been unraveling the mysteries of Earth for centuries—observing volcanoes, wondering what causes earthquakes, unearthing fossils, and prospecting for minerals. From their observations we have come to a better understanding of how our world works—from the hot, dense core of the planet to the surrounding envelope of air.

Planet Earth offers an up-to-date and easy-to-understand account of our physical world. In it you will read about the origins and structure of the Earth, how volcanoes erupt, and why continents drift. The major landscapes of the world are described, as are the oceans, the atmosphere and weather, and the Earth's resources. Essential facts and figures complete this comprehensive study of our extraordinary planet.

Neil Curtis

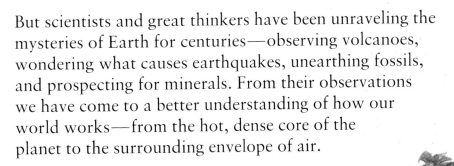

OUR PLANET

The Earth in Space

Viewed from space, the Earth appears as a round ball that shines bright and blue. People have not always seen the Earth in this way. Aristotle (384–322 B.C.), a philosopher in ancient Greece, and other scholars, believed that any problem could be solved by thinking carefully about it. He believed that the Earth was at the center of the universe, and that the Moon, Sun, planets, and stars orbited around it. You might come to the same conclusion if you lived on a desert island, with no radio, television, computers, or books, and no telescope to study the night sky. Indeed, you might not even guess you were on a spherical planet floating in space. At best, if you watched a ship disappearing beneath the horizon, you might figure out that the world's surface was curved. Today, we know that the Earth is one of a system of planets orbiting the Sun.

▶ *The Earth is not completely round. It is slightly flattened at the poles and bulges slightly at the equator. Clouds swirl continuously above the surface. Over two-thirds of the Earth is covered by water. Most of this water is contained in the oceans.*

EARTH DATAFILE

Diameter at the poles: 7,900 mi.
Diameter at the equator: 7,926 mi.
Circumference (distance around the Earth at the equator): 24,912 mi.
Volume: about 240 billion cu. mi.
Mass: 6.5 sextillion tons
Average density: 5.5 (water = 1)
Surface area: 197 million sq. mi.
Percentage of surface area covered by water: 71 percent
Age: 4.6 billion years
Age of the oldest known rocks: 3.7 billion years
Distance to the Moon: *maximum* 252,717 mi., *minimum* 221,462 mi.
Average distance to the Sun: 94 million mi.
Average thickness of the crust: 12 mi.
Average thickness of the mantle: 1,740 mi.
Average diameter of the core: 4,327 mi.
Temperature at the center: 8,132°F

▶ *Before modern mapping techniques, people had many different ideas about the Earth. These ideas included the belief that the Earth (and the Sun) were gods and that the Earth was flat.*

Egyptian Sun disk

15th century world map

Pluto · Neptune · Uranus · Saturn · Jupiter · Mars · Earth · Venus · Mercury · Sun

THE EARTH'S POSITION

Our Sun has a solar system of nine planets around it. The planets' characteristics are related to their distance from the Sun. Earth is one of the small inner planets, along with Mercury, Venus, and Mars. Closest to the Sun, Mercury and Venus are extremely hot. Each day on Mercury lasts over two Earth-months, during which its surface heats up to 842°F (450°C), and then cools to −274°F (−170°C) during the long night. Venus is even hotter, because of the greenhouse effect of its carbon dioxide atmosphere (see page 79). Next is Earth—the only planet with liquid water. Beyond Earth, Mars resembles a cold, red, stony desert. Colder still are the giant outer planets— Jupiter, Saturn, Uranus, and Neptune. They are made up partly of gases such as hydrogen and helium. Pluto is the smallest planet and is thought to be ice.

THE BIRTH OF THE EARTH

The Earth was formed at the same time as the Sun and the other planets in the Solar System. About 4.6 billion years ago, a rotating cloud of dust and gas, called a nebula, contracted under the pull of gravity. The pressure and temperature at the center of the nebula became so great it triggered a nuclear reaction. Some of the hydrogen in the cloud fused into helium, releasing great amounts of energy. This was the birth of the Sun. Farther from the center, material surrounding the Sun cooled and collided, building up into larger bodies. These eventually became the planets.

LINES ON EARTH

The Earth spins on an axis. The imaginary points on the Earth's surface where this axis projects are called the geographical poles.

The equator is an imaginary circle drawn around the Earth at an equal distance from the North and South poles. Imaginary circles drawn parallel to the equator are called lines of latitude. They are measured in degrees. The latitude of the equator is 0°, and the poles are 90° north and 90° south. Great circles drawn through the poles give lines of longitude. Zero longitude runs through Greenwich, London.

Greenwich Meridian · Line of latitude · Tropic of Cancer · Equator · Tropic of Capricorn · Line of longitude

▲ *Imaginary lines of latitude and longitude form a grid upon the Earth's surface for navigation and map-making. The tropics are two lines of latitude which mark the farthest limits where the Sun appears overhead.*

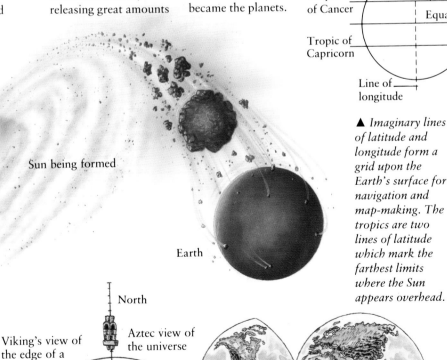

Nebula

Sun being formed

Earth

Viking's view of the edge of a flat Earth

North · Aztec view of the universe · West · Earth · East · South

Modern world map

Satellite image of the Earth

Gravity and the Earth

Gravity is the force of attraction that every object in the universe exerts on every other object. It is the weakest force known in physics, but its effects extend across the huge distances of space. The greater the mass of an object, the larger its gravitational attraction, but the farther away it is, the smaller the force. Gravitational forces are largely responsible for the orbits of bodies around the Sun and the orbit of our satellite, the Moon, around the Earth. These forces also give rise to the seasons and the tides.

THE EARTH'S DAY

The Earth's day is the time it takes to spin once on its axis (a little under 24 hours). If the Earth's axis were at right angles to its orbit, the length of a day would be the same all over the Earth. In fact, the Earth's axis is tilted by 23° 27′. This means that people in the hemisphere tilted toward the Sun see the Sun passing higher across the sky, and daylength is longer. The hemisphere tilted away from the Sun has a shorter day.

► *Twice a year, usually on March 21 and September 22, day and night are of equal length all over the Earth.*

THE EARTH'S YEAR

The Earth's year is the time it takes for the Earth to complete one orbit of the Sun (365 days, 5 hours, 48 minutes, and 46 seconds). The year is divided into 365 days, but every fourth year, a leap year, has 366 days to make up the extra time. In a leap year February has 29 days.

THE SEASONS

Since the Earth's axis is tilted, the hemispheres are at different angles to the Sun. This phenomenon gives rise to the seasons. In winter the days are short and cold and in summer they are long and warm. At the equator, daylength varies little throughout the year, and the seasons are linked to rainfall.

Sun

21 December
Winter begins in
Northern Hemisphere,
summer begins in
Southern Hemisphere

21 March
Spring begins in
Northern Hemisphere,
autumn in Southern
Hemisphere

21 June
Summer begins in
Northern Hemisphere
winter begins in
Southern Hemisphere

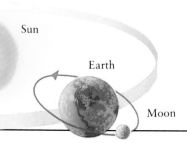

Sun

Earth

Moon

▲ *In the Northern Hemisphere, summer begins officially on June 21, the longest day of the year. In the Southern Hemisphere June 21 is the shortest day.*

THE PULL OF GRAVITY

The sea rises and falls every 12 hours and 26 minutes. These tides are caused by the gravity of the Moon, and also the Sun. The Moon's gravity pulls the oceans on the side of the Earth nearer to it more than it pulls the Earth itself, causing a bulge of water, or tide. On the opposite side, the Earth is pulled more than the oceans, and this leaves behind a slightly smaller bulge of water.

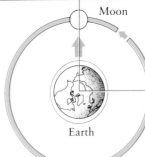
Moon

Sun

Earth

▲ *When the Sun and Moon are at right angles and pulling in different directions, the lowest tides take place. These are called neap tides.*

Moon   Sun

Earth

▲ *When the Sun and Moon are in line, pulling together—at new or full moon—high tides, known as spring tides, occur.*

23 September
Autumn begins in
Northern Hemisphere,
spring begins in
Southern Hemisphere

◄ *The Bay of Fundy, Canada, boasts the world's greatest spring tidal range—47.5 ft. (14.5 m) between high and low tides.*

THE EARTH'S ENERGY BALANCE

The Sun radiates (gives out) energy and can be thought of as the Earth's power plant. It supplies the energy that drives the Earth's climate and weather. It is the energy source for all plant life and, therefore, for all animal life as well. At a temperature of some 27 million °F (15 million °C), the Sun's fuel source, hydrogen, fuses into helium (the hydrogen atoms combine to form helium atoms) and releases energy. Our planet receives just one two-billionth of the energy that the Sun generates.

Radiation
from Sun

▶ *Thirty percent of the available radiation is reflected directly back into space by clouds, or by the surface of the planet.*

▼ *Radiation reflected by the Earth is absorbed by gases in the atmosphere such as carbon dioxide. The energy is then radiated again, some of it returning to Earth.*

Radiation
reflected
back to space

Radiation
reflected
to Earth's
surface

Absorption
by atmosphere

▶ *About 70 percent of the Sun's radiation that reaches the Earth is absorbed and then radiated back again. Of this 70 percent, 25 percent is absorbed by the atmosphere and the rest by the planet itself.*

The Structure of the Earth

Although earthquakes can have catastrophic effects, they can also reveal a great deal about the Earth's structure. The shock waves pass through the Earth in different ways and can be recorded by scientists using sensitive instruments called seismometers. Scientists have been able to identify three main zones according to their densities: the thin outer crust, the mantle, and the core in the center. The upper layers of the Earth are also categorized as the lithosphere, hydrosphere, and asthenosphere.

▼ *The Earth's crust is divided into oceanic crust and continental crust, both of which originate in the mantle. The thicker continental crust can vary from about 22 mi. (35 km) thick to as much as 31 mi. (50 km) beneath mountain ranges. It is made mainly from pale, granitelike rocks.*

▼ *The lithosphere is the upper, rocky layer of the Earth. It includes the crust and the top, brittle part of the mantle; it can be up to 186 mi. (300 km) thick.*

▼ *The hydrosphere is the water (mainly the oceans and seas) on the Earth's surface. After the Earth was formed, water vapor in the atmosphere condensed to form the hydrosphere.*

▶ *The thinner rocky crust beneath the oceans is only about 3 mi. (5 km) thick. It is made up mainly of dark rocks called basalt and gabbro and has been formed in the last 200 million years.*

▶ *The asthenosphere is the layer of the mantle beneath the lithosphere which is in an almost fluid or "plastic" state, so that it behaves like an extremely thick liquid.*

THE MOHOLE PROJECT
Rocks on the surface of the Earth can easily be examined. But the inside of the planet is hidden from scientists, except when volcanic eruptions spew out material. The boundary between the crust and the mantle is called the Mohorovičić discontinuity, after a Croatian scientist. In the 1960s, an attempt was made to drill through the ocean crust to take samples of the mantle. The "Mohole" project was abandoned because of increasing costs.

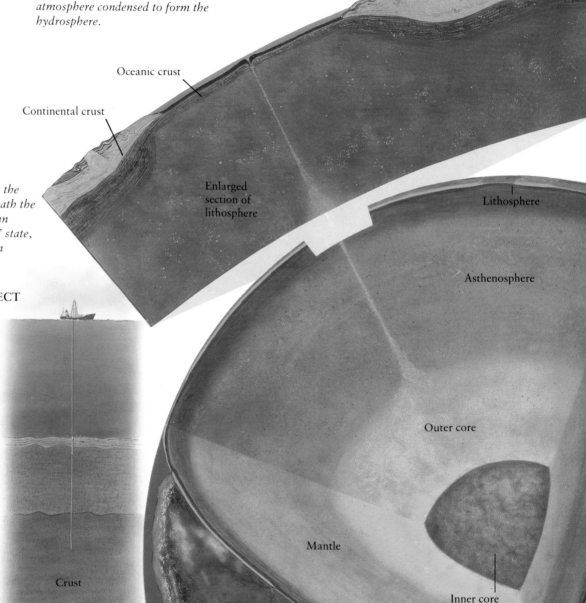

Oceanic crust

Continental crust

Enlarged section of lithosphere

Lithosphere

Asthenosphere

Outer core

Mantle

Inner core

Crust

Crust

Mantle

MAGNETIC ATTRACTION

The Earth's magnetic field extends far into space. The Sun showers the Earth with charged atomic particles —the solar wind—which are affected by the Earth's magnetic field, or the magnetosphere. In places where the magnetosphere is dense, the atomic particles are trapped in two layers around the Earth. These layers are called the Van Allen belts.

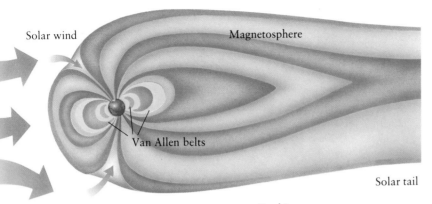

Solar wind

Magnetosphere

Van Allen belts

Solar tail

Solar wind

Earth's magnetic field

Lines of force

◀ *The Earth is magnetic and behaves somewhat like a bar magnet with a magnetic field. The Earth's magnetic poles and the geographic poles do not exactly coincide.*

THE EARTH'S MAGNETISM

Homing pigeon

Magnetism is a property of materials such as iron, and of electric currents, in which moving charged particles develop a force of attraction. The Earth is magnetic and has magnetic poles and a magnetic field. If a magnetized needle is floated in a bowl of water it will align itself with the Earth's magnetic poles. This is a simple compass and can be used for navigation, although the difference between the geographic poles and the magnetic poles (magnetic variation) must be taken into account. Magnetic variation changes over time. It appears that the magnetic poles are "wandering," but it is actually the continents that are moving over them.

Some animals, such as pigeons, have been shown to use the Earth's magnetic field to navigate. If they are released in areas where there is some kind of magnetic disturbance, homing pigeons seem to lose their way.

Magnetic compass

◀ *The aurora australis, or the southern lights, is a "curtain" of spectacular lights in the sky at the South Pole. They are caused by the collision of the solar wind with the Earth's atmosphere. The aurora borealis occurs at the North Pole.*

THE CORE AND MANTLE

Lying beneath the Earth's crust, the mantle is about 1,740 mi. (2,800 km) thick. It is made of rock. The central zone of the Earth is called the core. It is divided into inner and outer zones. The inner core is solid, but the outer core is liquid. Both are dense and hot and consist mainly of nickel and iron.

THE CRUST

These are the main elements that make up the crust:

Oxygen	Calcium
Silicon	Sodium
Aluminum	Potassium
Iron	Magnesium

Land, Water, and Air

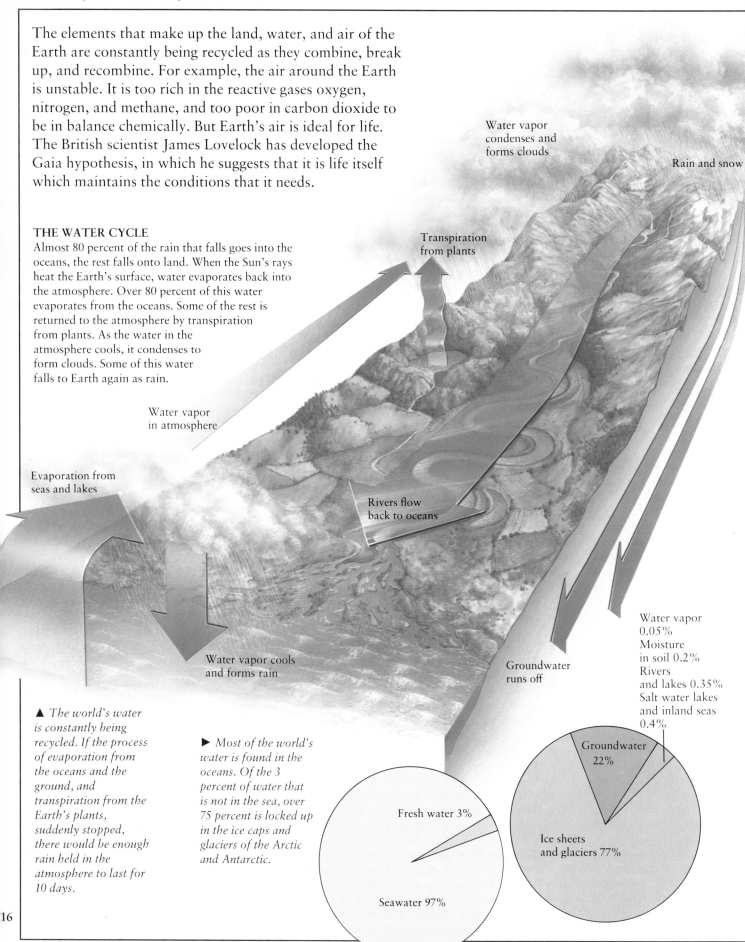

The elements that make up the land, water, and air of the Earth are constantly being recycled as they combine, break up, and recombine. For example, the air around the Earth is unstable. It is too rich in the reactive gases oxygen, nitrogen, and methane, and too poor in carbon dioxide to be in balance chemically. But Earth's air is ideal for life. The British scientist James Lovelock has developed the Gaia hypothesis, in which he suggests that it is life itself which maintains the conditions that it needs.

THE WATER CYCLE

Almost 80 percent of the rain that falls goes into the oceans, the rest falls onto land. When the Sun's rays heat the Earth's surface, water evaporates back into the atmosphere. Over 80 percent of this water evaporates from the oceans. Some of the rest is returned to the atmosphere by transpiration from plants. As the water in the atmosphere cools, it condenses to form clouds. Some of this water falls to Earth again as rain.

Water vapor
in atmosphere

Evaporation from
seas and lakes

Water vapor cools
and forms rain

▲ *The world's water is constantly being recycled. If the process of evaporation from the oceans and the ground, and transpiration from the Earth's plants, suddenly stopped, there would be enough rain held in the atmosphere to last for 10 days.*

▶ *Most of the world's water is found in the oceans. Of the 3 percent of water that is not in the sea, over 75 percent is locked up in the ice caps and glaciers of the Arctic and Antarctic.*

Water vapor
condenses and
forms clouds

Rain and snow

Transpiration
from plants

Rivers flow
back to oceans

Groundwater
runs off

Water vapor
0.05%
Moisture
in soil 0.2%
Rivers
and lakes 0.35%
Salt water lakes
and inland seas
0.4%

Groundwater
22%

Ice sheets
and glaciers 77%

Fresh water 3%

Seawater 97%

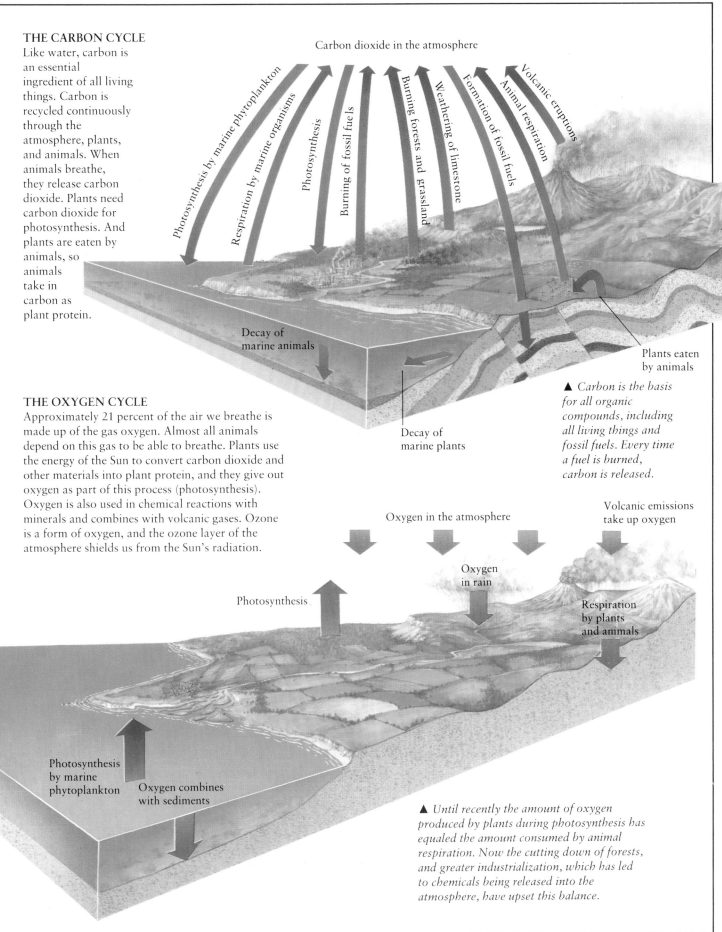

THE CARBON CYCLE

Like water, carbon is an essential ingredient of all living things. Carbon is recycled continuously through the atmosphere, plants, and animals. When animals breathe, they release carbon dioxide. Plants need carbon dioxide for photosynthesis. And plants are eaten by animals, so animals take in carbon as plant protein.

Carbon dioxide in the atmosphere

Photosynthesis by marine phytoplankton

Respiration by marine organisms

Photosynthesis

Burning of fossil fuels

Burning forests and grassland

Weathering of limestone

Formation of fossil fuels

Animal respiration

Volcanic eruptions

Decay of marine animals

Decay of marine plants

Plants eaten by animals

▲ *Carbon is the basis for all organic compounds, including all living things and fossil fuels. Every time a fuel is burned, carbon is released.*

THE OXYGEN CYCLE

Approximately 21 percent of the air we breathe is made up of the gas oxygen. Almost all animals depend on this gas to be able to breathe. Plants use the energy of the Sun to convert carbon dioxide and other materials into plant protein, and they give out oxygen as part of this process (photosynthesis). Oxygen is also used in chemical reactions with minerals and combines with volcanic gases. Ozone is a form of oxygen, and the ozone layer of the atmosphere shields us from the Sun's radiation.

Oxygen in the atmosphere

Volcanic emissions take up oxygen

Oxygen in rain

Photosynthesis

Respiration by plants and animals

Photosynthesis by marine phytoplankton

Oxygen combines with sediments

▲ *Until recently the amount of oxygen produced by plants during photosynthesis has equaled the amount consumed by animal respiration. Now the cutting down of forests, and greater industrialization, which has led to chemicals being released into the atmosphere, have upset this balance.*

THE LAND

Earthquakes

Earthquakes are among the most serious natural disasters: the ground shakes and may crack; poorly constructed buildings collapse; dams are destroyed; huge ocean waves flood the land; gas mains rupture; and fires break out. Many hundreds or even thousands of people may be killed or left homeless as a result.

Earthquakes occur because within the Earth's asthenosphere, stress causes the semiplastic rocks to move very slowly. This builds up strain within the more brittle rocks of the lithosphere above. Eventually, the brittle rocks break and the stress is released as shock waves. Earthquakes can take place at depths of up to 450 mi. (720 km). But those that have effects at the surface usually occur no deeper than 45 mi. (70 km). Every year there are about 1,000 earthquakes around the world that are strong enough to cause some damage.

SHOCK WAVES
When a rock within the lithosphere fractures it sends out shock waves in all directions. The source of these waves is called the hypocenter of the quake. The point on the surface above the source is the epicenter.

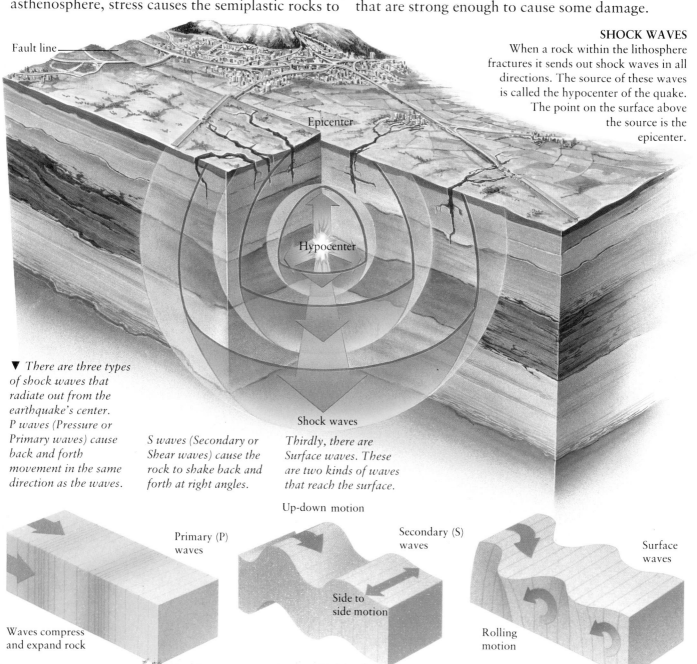

Fault line

Epicenter

Hypocenter

Shock waves

▼ *There are three types of shock waves that radiate out from the earthquake's center. P waves (Pressure or Primary waves) cause back and forth movement in the same direction as the waves.*

S waves (Secondary or Shear waves) cause the rock to shake back and forth at right angles.

Thirdly, there are Surface waves. These are two kinds of waves that reach the surface.

Up-down motion

Primary (P) waves

Secondary (S) waves

Side to side motion

Surface waves

Waves compress and expand rock

Rolling motion

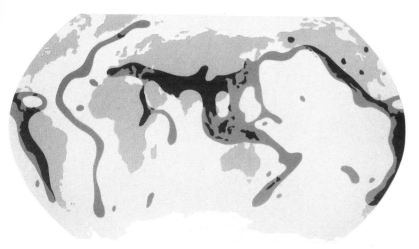

EARTHQUAKE ZONES

Scientists continuously monitor earthquakes and plot the sites of major quakes on a map. A distinct pattern has emerged showing that, with a few exceptions, earthquakes take place in a number of definite zones. Earthquakes happen where there are deep trenches in the ocean bed with groups of islands nearby, such as around the Pacific.

In earthquake areas, seismologists try to figure out whether stress is building up in the rocks. If the area is quiet for a long time, it may be that stress is building up and may eventually cause a major earthquake. Seismologists can also use one or more seismometers to detect the tiny shock waves that occur before an earthquake.

Earthquake zones

▲ When an earthquake takes place under the seabed, it may produce a wave in the sea. In the open ocean the wave may hardly be noticed. But if it reaches shallow water near a coast, the wave may rise to heights of 100 ft. (30 m) or more. These giant waves are called tsunamis.

EARTHQUAKE SCALES

The intensity of earthquakes is measured on two scales. The Mercalli scale, based on observable effects, ranges from "not felt" at 1 to "total devastation" at scale 12. The Richter scale is based on the size of the shock waves produced.

Mercalli and Richter Scales

1	< 3	Very slight: detected by instruments only
2	3–3.4	Feeble: felt by people resting
3	3.5–4	Slight: like heavy trucks passing
4	4.1–4.4	Moderate: windows rattle
5	4.5–4.8	Rather strong: wakes sleeping people
6	4.9–5.4	Strong: trees sway, walls crack
7	5.5–6	Very strong: people fall over, buildings crack
8	6.1–6.5	Destructive: chimneys fall, buildings move
9	6.6–7	Ruinous: heavy damage to buildings, ground cracks
10	7.1–7.3	Disastrous: most buildings destroyed, landslides
11	7.4–8.1	Very disastrous: railroads and pipelines break
12	> 8.1	Catastrophic: total devastation

EARTHQUAKE DAMAGE

If a large earthquake occurs where people live then there may be casualties as buildings collapse. Fire has always been a hazard, originally as buildings fell on domestic fires and burned, and now as gas mains break and catch fire.

▲ In 1906, the San Andreas fault moved 21.3 ft. (6.5 m), causing an earthquake that destroyed San Francisco. Much of the city burned down as gas mains broke and caught fire.

Trans-America Pyramid, San Francisco

PREVENTING COLLAPSE

When an earthquake strikes, badly built houses collapse. It is, however, possible to construct buildings, even skyscrapers, that will resist collapse. Earthquake-proof buildings must have their foundations built into the solid rock, and they must be able to bend without shattering.

Volcanoes

A volcano is any kind of fissure, or natural opening, in the Earth's crust through which hot molten rock (called lava), ash, steam, gas, and other material is spewed. The heat comes from within the Earth's mantle. The word "volcano" (after Vulcan, the Roman god of fire and metalworking) is also used to describe the cone of lava and ash that builds up around the opening. The shape depends on the type of eruption. Volcanic activity may take place under the sea as well as on land, and it sometimes creates new land.

TYPES OF VOLCANOES

Peléan eruption

Hawaiian eruption

▲ Mount Pelé is a volcano on Martinique, West Indies. In an explosive Peléan eruption the lava is thick and the volcano gives out glowing, gas-charged clouds.

▲ The cones created by a Hawaiian eruption are big at the bottom and slope gently because the lava, which pours out in fountains, is quite runny.

Strombolian eruption

▲ Stromboli is an active volcano on an island north of Sicily. A Strombolian eruption occurs regularly, but with small explosions.

Plinian eruption

Vulcanian eruption

▲ Pliny the Elder died in A.D. 79 when Vesuvius erupted and the Roman city of Pompeii was destroyed. A Plinian eruption is explosive with great clouds of ash and volcanic rock, or pumice. A vulcanian eruption (left), after Vulcano, near Stromboli, is characterized by rare explosions of almost solid magma thrown long distances.

► Sometimes, a volcano may explode very violently, emptying the lava chamber that feeds it. The roof and walls may then collapse, leaving a hole called a caldera.

Ash and smoke

INSIDE A VOLCANO

A typical volcano, with a crater and a cone of solidified lava and ash, is called a central type. The activity takes place in a chimneylike "pipe," or vent, through which the material erupts. Far below the vent is a chamber of molten rock (magma) containing dissolved gases. Gas bubbling out of the magma keeps the vent open. Sometimes, lava and other material may break through farther down the sides of the volcano, and a secondary or parasite core is formed.

Caldera

Lava flow

FAMOUS ERUPTIONS
Eruptions occur when the pressure in the chamber and vent has built up and the material breaks through.

Mt. Etna, Sicily, 1669

Mt. St. Helens, Wash., 1980

Taupa, New Zealand, A.D. 130

Cotopaxi, Ecuador, 1877

Mauna, Loa, Hawaii, 1872

Vesuvius, Italy A.D. 79

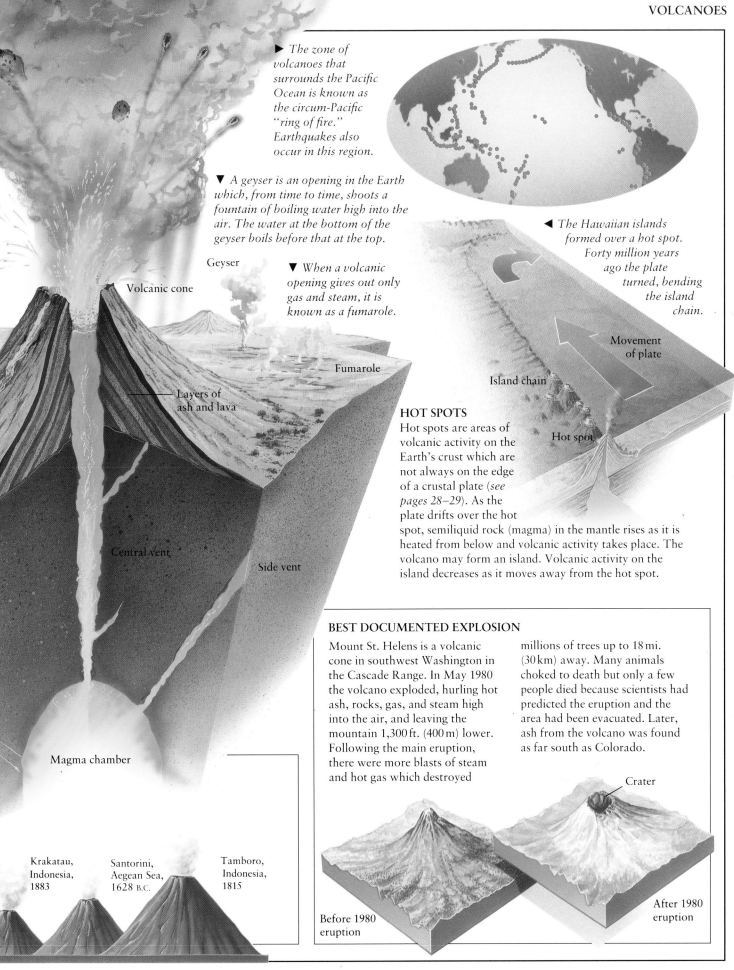

▶ *The zone of volcanoes that surrounds the Pacific Ocean is known as the circum-Pacific "ring of fire." Earthquakes also occur in this region.*

▼ *A geyser is an opening in the Earth which, from time to time, shoots a fountain of boiling water high into the air. The water at the bottom of the geyser boils before that at the top.*

Geyser

Volcanic cone

▼ *When a volcanic opening gives out only gas and steam, it is known as a fumarole.*

Fumarole

Layers of ash and lava

Central vent

Side vent

Magma chamber

◀ *The Hawaiian islands formed over a hot spot. Forty million years ago the plate turned, bending the island chain.*

Movement of plate

Island chain

Hot spot

HOT SPOTS

Hot spots are areas of volcanic activity on the Earth's crust which are not always on the edge of a crustal plate (*see pages 28–29*). As the plate drifts over the hot spot, semiliquid rock (magma) in the mantle rises as it is heated from below and volcanic activity takes place. The volcano may form an island. Volcanic activity on the island decreases as it moves away from the hot spot.

BEST DOCUMENTED EXPLOSION

Mount St. Helens is a volcanic cone in southwest Washington in the Cascade Range. In May 1980 the volcano exploded, hurling hot ash, rocks, gas, and steam high into the air, and leaving the mountain 1,300 ft. (400 m) lower. Following the main eruption, there were more blasts of steam and hot gas which destroyed millions of trees up to 18 mi. (30 km) away. Many animals choked to death but only a few people died because scientists had predicted the eruption and the area had been evacuated. Later, ash from the volcano was found as far south as Colorado.

Crater

Krakatau, Indonesia, 1883

Santorini, Aegean Sea, 1628 B.C.

Tamboro, Indonesia, 1815

Before 1980 eruption

After 1980 eruption

21

Drifting Continents

The coastlines of eastern South America and West Africa could fit together like pieces in a jigsaw. This match was noticed in the 17th century. However, it was not until 1912 that Alfred Wegener proposed that all the land masses of the world had originally formed one super-continent, which he called Pangaea. This could not be explained until the early 1960s, when scientists discovered that the rocky plates of the Earth's lithosphere were moving, floating on the more mobile rock below.

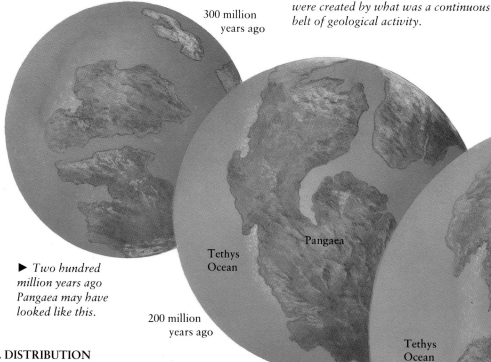

▶ As well as the matching coastlines, there is other evidence that there was once a single continent. There are remains of an ancient mountain belt, between 470 and 350 million years old, which are now separated by the Atlantic Ocean. These mountains were created by what was a continuous belt of geological activity.

Africa
South America
India
Antarctica
Australia
Fold mountains

300 million years ago

200 million years ago

65 million years ago

Tethys Ocean

Pangaea

Laurasia

Tethys Ocean

Gondwanaland

EVOLVING EARTH

The supercontinent, Pangaea, is thought to have evolved some 280 million years ago, at the end of the Carboniferous Period. By mid-Jurassic times, 150 million years ago, Pangaea had split into a northern continent, Laurasia, and a southern continent, Gondwanaland. By the end of the Cretaceous, about 65 million years ago, Gondwanaland was breaking up, although North America had not yet split from Eurasia.

▶ Two hundred million years ago Pangaea may have looked like this.

PLANT AND ANIMAL DISTRIBUTION

Some fossils also tell us that the continents were once joined. For example, fossils of the plant *Glossopteris* and the animals *Mesosaurus* and *Lystrosaurus* have all been found in the southern continents, which are now widely separated.

Africa
South America
India
Antarctica
Australia

 Lystrosaurus

 Mesosaurus

 Glossopteris

▲ Some very similar species exist far apart. This marsupial opposum lives in North America, whereas most marsupials live in Australasia.

Mesosaurus

22

TODAY

The present distribution of the continents has taken place in the last 65 million years. Today, the drift still continues. The Atlantic Ocean is getting wider by a few inches a year, the Pacific Ocean is getting smaller, and the Red Sea is part of a crack in the crust that will widen to produce a new ocean millions of years in the future.

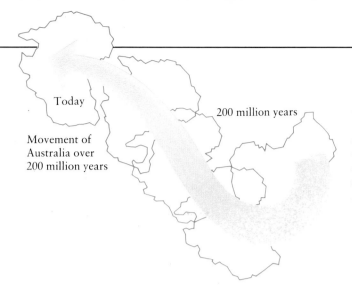

Today

Movement of Australia over 200 million years

200 million years

◄ *Australia has nearly turned completely around from its original position and is now moving northward. In 50 million years time it will be touching the landmass of Eurasia.*

Today

▼ *The world begins to look more familiar 65 million years ago. The widening South Atlantic Ocean has separated Africa and South America, and Madagascar has split from Africa, but Australia and Antarctica are still joined.*

25 million years ago

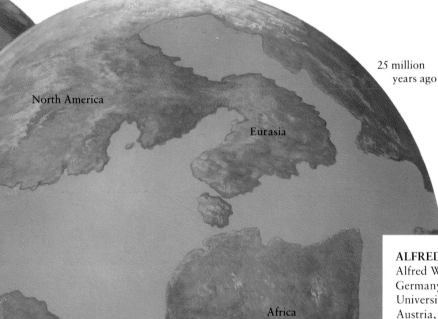

North America

Eurasia

Africa

South America

ALFRED WEGENER (1880–1930)

Alfred Wegener was born in Berlin, Germany. He studied meteorology at the Universities of Heidelberg, Innsbruck in Austria, and in Berlin. In 1924 he returned to Graz, Austria, to become professor of meteorology and geophysics.

In 1910 the American scientist F. B. Taylor put forward the idea that whole continents could have drifted across the surface of the planet. This theory was taken up in 1911 by H. B. Baker and then by Wegener in 1912, who developed his theory of continental drift known as the Wegener hypothesis. He published *Origins of Continents and Oceans* in which he explained his ideas. Wegener also suggested that, with the shifting land masses, the magnetic poles moved around. He died in Greenland on his fourth expedition there.

Plate Tectonics

The word "tectonics" comes from the Greek *tekton*, meaning "builder." The theory suggests that the surface of the Earth is made up of rigid plates of lithosphere which "float" on the more mobile asthenosphere. Owing to movements in the asthenosphere, the plates are in constant motion. It explains many of the major processes of the Earth, such as the drifting of continents, mountain building, and earthquake and volcanic activity. Much of this activity occurs at the edges, or margins, of the plates.

▶ *Movements of the plates of lithosphere may be driven by convection currents in the asthenosphere. Hot currents rise, then cool as they reach the surface. At the same time, cooler currents sink. This movement carries the crustal plates.*

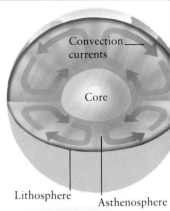

Convection currents

Core

Lithosphere

Asthenosphere

SEAFLOOR SPREADING

Down the middle of the Atlantic Ocean floor is a ridge where volcanic activity takes place. This ridge marks a plate margin. Along the ridge are cracks where molten rocks push up to form new crust. The crust spreads away from the ridge, and the ocean basin widens.

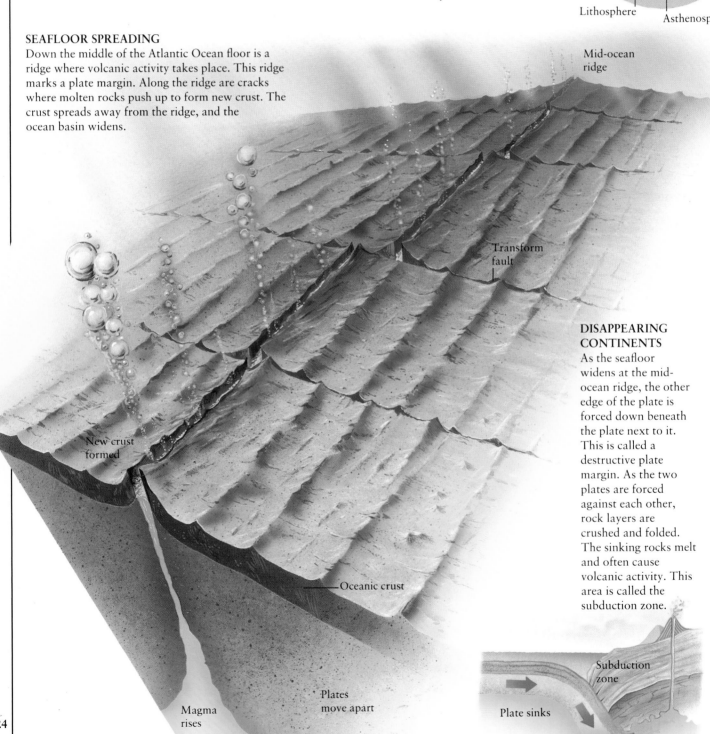

Mid-ocean ridge

Transform fault

New crust formed

Oceanic crust

Magma rises

Plates move apart

DISAPPEARING CONTINENTS

As the seafloor widens at the mid-ocean ridge, the other edge of the plate is forced down beneath the plate next to it. This is called a destructive plate margin. As the two plates are forced against each other, rock layers are crushed and folded. The sinking rocks melt and often cause volcanic activity. This area is called the subduction zone.

Subduction zone

Plate sinks

ICELAND

Iceland is situated on the mid-Atlantic ridge between Greenland and Scandinavia. It was formed from eruptions from the ridge and is still getting wider by 1 in. (2.5 cm) a year. This activity means that it is a volcanic island, with geysers and hot springs.

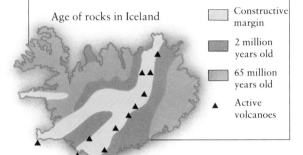

Age of rocks in Iceland

☐	Constructive margin
☐	2 million years old
☐	65 million years old
▲	Active volcanoes

OCEANS AND CONTINENTS

All oceanic crust is less than 200 million years old. It has four main layers. The top layer is made up of sand and mud laid down in the world's seas. Beneath it is a layer of basalt. Then comes a layer of another dark rock called gabbro, and finally a thin layer above the mantle. Oceanic crust is about 7 mi. (11 km) thick.

The thicker continental crust has only two layers: the upper one is mainly granite, with gabbro beneath. On average, continental crust is about 22 mi. (35 km) thick, but may be 31 mi. (50 km) thick under recently built mountains.

▶ *The crust that forms the continents is far thicker than that under the oceans.*

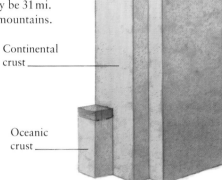

Andes Mountains

Montana

Continental crust

Oceanic crust

◀ *The Earth's crust is made up of eight main plates and several smaller ones. The edges of these plates are marked by ridges and trenches. New crust is formed at the ridges and destroyed at the trenches. Large faults, known as transform faults, occur at right angles to the mid-oceanic ridges. As new crust is created in the mid-Atlantic, the North American and South American plates are moving westward. India continues to move northward; as it collides with the Eurasian plate, which is traveling eastward, the Himalayas get higher. The African plate continues its drift to the northwest as the Red Sea opens up.*

NORTH AMERICAN PLATE

Mid-Atlantic Ridge

EURASIAN PLATE

Japan Trench

COCOS PLATE

CARIBBEAN PLATE

AFRICAN PLATE

PACIFIC PLATE

SOUTH AMERICAN PLATE

Java Trench

NAZCA PLATE

East Pacific Rise

Mid-Indian Ridge

INDO-AUSTRALIAN PLATE

ANTARCTIC PLATE

—·— Plate margin

Transform faults

▶ *Running from the northeast of Scotland to the southwest, a series of lochs follows the line of the Great Glen. This valley is a good example of a tear fault (see page 28). Some 400 million years ago, the land north of the fault slid southwest by 60 mi. (100 km).*

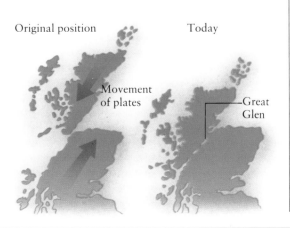

Original position

Today

Movement of plates

Great Glen

FACTS ABOUT PLATE TECTONICS

● When lavas cool and harden into rock, some minerals are magnetized in the direction of the Earth's magnetic poles at that time. About every 400,000–500,000 years, the Earth's magnetic poles reverse.
● By measuring the ages and magnetism of rocks on either side of the mid-Atlantic ridge, geologists have proved that the Atlantic is widening.
● The Atlantic widens by 0.4–2 in. a year.
● It has taken about 200 million years to separate South America from Africa and create the Atlantic Ocean, and about 40 million years for Australia and the Antarctic to move apart to their present positions.

Mountains

A mountain is an area of high ground that is higher (over 1,000 ft. [300 m]) than a hill. A group of mountains is called a range. The greatest mountain ranges are the European Alps, the Andes of South America, the Rockies of North America, and—the highest of all—the Himalayas of Asia. It takes millions of years for mountains to be formed. The process is going on continuously as sections of the Earth's crust are thrust, folded, and broken, pushing up rocks to make new mountains.

HOW MOUNTAINS ARE FORMED
The surface of the Earth is made up of giant slow-moving plates of crust and mantle. Where two continental plates collide, a mountain belt is thrust slowly upward. The sediments of the ocean floor are squeezed into folds, which may be tens of thousands of feet high. The folds may then be overturned, one on top of the other. Beneath the chain of mountains is a thick layer of continental crust.

THE HIMALAYAS
The high mountains of the Himalayas mark a region of the Earth's crust where two continental plates are colliding. The Indo-Australian plate is pushing north into the Eurasian plate. Eventually the two continents will become locked together.

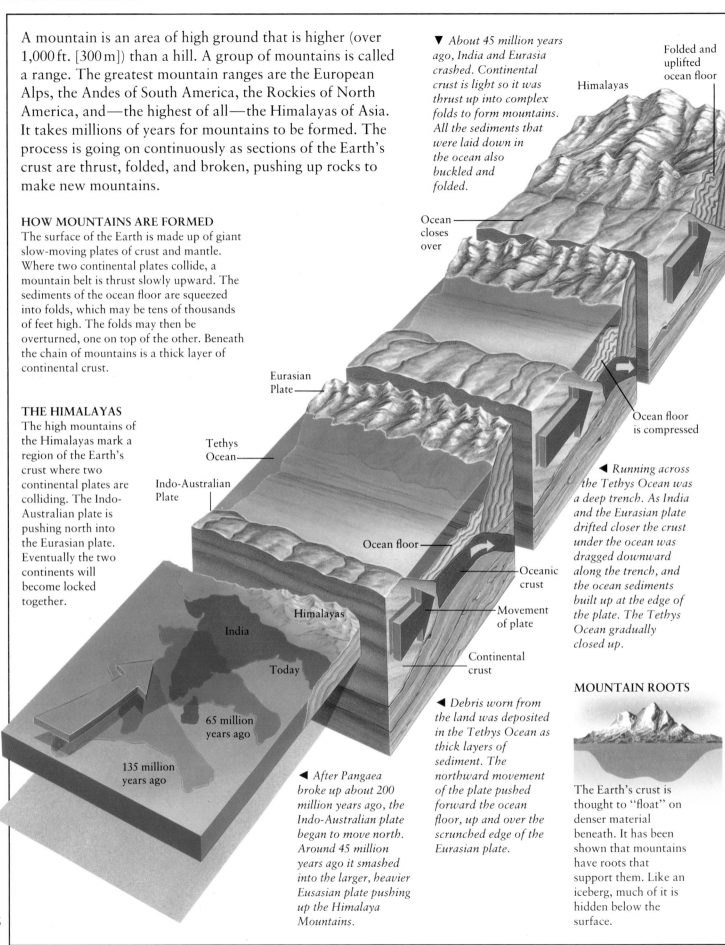

▼ About 45 million years ago, India and Eurasia crashed. Continental crust is light so it was thrust up into complex folds to form mountains. All the sediments that were laid down in the ocean also buckled and folded.

Folded and uplifted ocean floor

Himalayas

Ocean closes over

Eurasian Plate

Tethys Ocean

Indo-Australian Plate

Ocean floor

Ocean floor is compressed

◄ Running across the Tethys Ocean was a deep trench. As India and the Eurasian plate drifted closer the crust under the ocean was dragged downward along the trench, and the ocean sediments built up at the edge of the plate. The Tethys Ocean gradually closed up.

Oceanic crust

Movement of plate

Continental crust

India

Himalayas

Today

65 million years ago

135 million years ago

◄ Debris worn from the land was deposited in the Tethys Ocean as thick layers of sediment. The northward movement of the plate pushed forward the ocean floor, up and over the scrunched edge of the Eurasian plate.

◄ After Pangaea broke up about 200 million years ago, the Indo-Australian plate began to move north. Around 45 million years ago it smashed into the larger, heavier Eusasian plate pushing up the Himalaya Mountains.

MOUNTAIN ROOTS

The Earth's crust is thought to "float" on denser material beneath. It has been shown that mountains have roots that support them. Like an iceberg, much of it is hidden below the surface.

▲ *The shape of a mountain depends on how it was formed, its age, and how much it has been eroded and worn. Young mountains, such as the Himalayas, are high and rugged. Old mountains are smoother and lower.*

MOUNTAIN BELTS

Eventually, weathering wears away the crumpled and faulted rocks of a mountain range. Some rocks resist weathering better than others. Those that do may survive for longer as high, jagged peaks.

MOUNTAIN LIFE

Different animals and plants live in different zones, or areas, of a mountain. Many cannot survive the extreme cold and thin air at high altitudes, but flourish on the lower slopes. The types of animals and plants that live in each of the zones vary in different mountain ranges. In warm equatorial regions, trees may be able to live at 13,000 ft. (4,000 m). But in the colder Alps, trees can survive only up to 6,000 ft. (1,800 m).

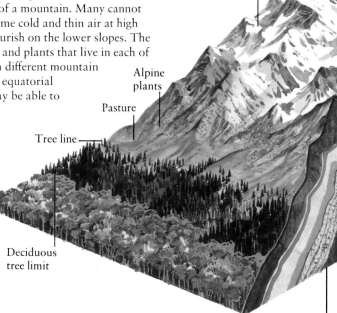

Snow field
Alpine plants
Pasture
Tree line
Deciduous tree limit

MAJOR MOUNTAIN RANGES

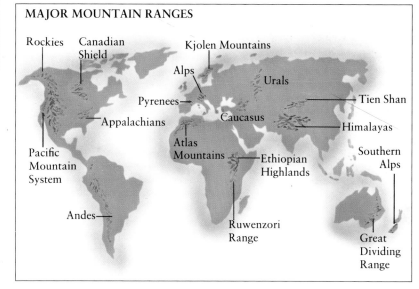

Rockies
Canadian Shield
Kjolen Mountains
Alps
Urals
Pyrenees
Tien Shan
Appalachians
Caucasus
Himalayas
Pacific Mountain System
Atlas Mountains
Ethiopian Highlands
Southern Alps
Andes
Ruwenzori Range
Great Dividing Range

MOUNTAIN DATAFILE

The world's highest peaks (14 over 24,000 ft. [8,000 m]) are in the Himalaya-Karakoram ranges.

Top 5 in Asia
1 Mount Everest
  29,028 ft. (8,848 m)
2 Godwin-Austin (K2)
  28,250 ft. (8,611 m)
3 Kanchenjunga
  28,208 ft. (8,597 m)
4 Makalu
  27,824 ft. (8,480 m)
5 Dhaulagiri
  26,810 ft. (8,172 m)

Highest in other continents
6 Aconcagua (South America)
  22,831 ft. (6,959 m)
7 McKinley (North America)
  20,320 ft. (6,194 m)
8 Kilimanjaro (Africa)
  19,340 ft. (5,895 m)
9 Elbrus (Europe)
  18,481 ft. (5,633 m)
10 Vinson Massif (Antarctica)
  16,860 ft. (5,139 m)
11 Mt. Wilhelm (Oceania)
  14,793 ft. (4,509 m)

▶ *Mountaineering began as a sport in the mid-1800s, when British and other European climbers tried to scale the peaks of the Alps. On May 29, 1953, mountaineering history was made when the New Zealander Edmund Hillary (1919–) and his Sherpa guide, Tenzing Norgay (1914–86), reached the summit of Mount Everest, the world's highest peak. In 1975, the Japanese climber Junko Tabei (1939–) became the first woman to climb Everest.*

27

Bending and Breaking

If you hit a rock hard enough with a hammer, it will break. It is harder to imagine rocks bending. But when movements in the Earth cause stress to build up over a long period of time, the layers of rock may break or bend. A break in the rocks is known as a fault. When rock layers bend into waves, or sometimes overturn until they are upside-down, they are said to have folded. There are different kinds of folds and faults, depending on the type of rock and the force that has pushed or pulled it.

FOLDS BEFORE FAULTS

If you take several layers of paper, hold them by the edges and then push, they will bend into a dome. If you try the same experiment with some cardboard, it will probably not bend as easily, and may break. Rocks can behave more like the paper than the cardboard. When they are pushed or pulled, they may recover if the stress is removed. But if the rock is brittle and is deformed too much it will break. It will bend if it is more elastic.

THE PARTS OF A FAULT

The angle made by the fault and the horizontal is called the dip. If the angle is measured from the vertical it is called the hade. The relative movements of the blocks of rock on either side of the fault are known as its slip; the vertical movement when the blocks have slipped up or down the dip is the throw.

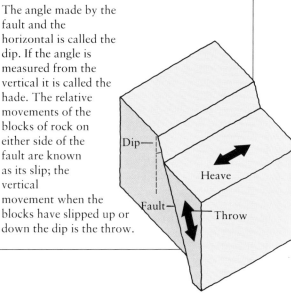

Normal fault

Reverse fault

Strike-slip fault

Rock strata

Movement of rock

A normal fault occurs when a block of rock on one side of the fault has slipped down the slope of the fault.

When a block on one side of the fault is forced up the slope of the fault, it is called a reverse fault.

In a transcurrent fault (or strike-slip fault) the main movement is horizontal when the beds of rock are horizontal.

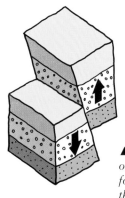

Oblique fault

An oblique fault resembles a combination of a transcurrent fault with either a normal or a reverse fault. The amounts of movement in each direction are similar.

Sandstone and shale beds in this cliff have been crushed into folds, and then shifted onto one end by the movement of the Earth's crust.

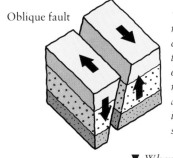

When a block of rock has been thrown upward between two steeply angled faults, it is called a horst.

Graben

Horst

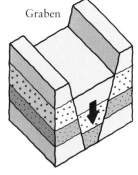

A graben is a down-thrown block of rock between two steeply angled normal faults.

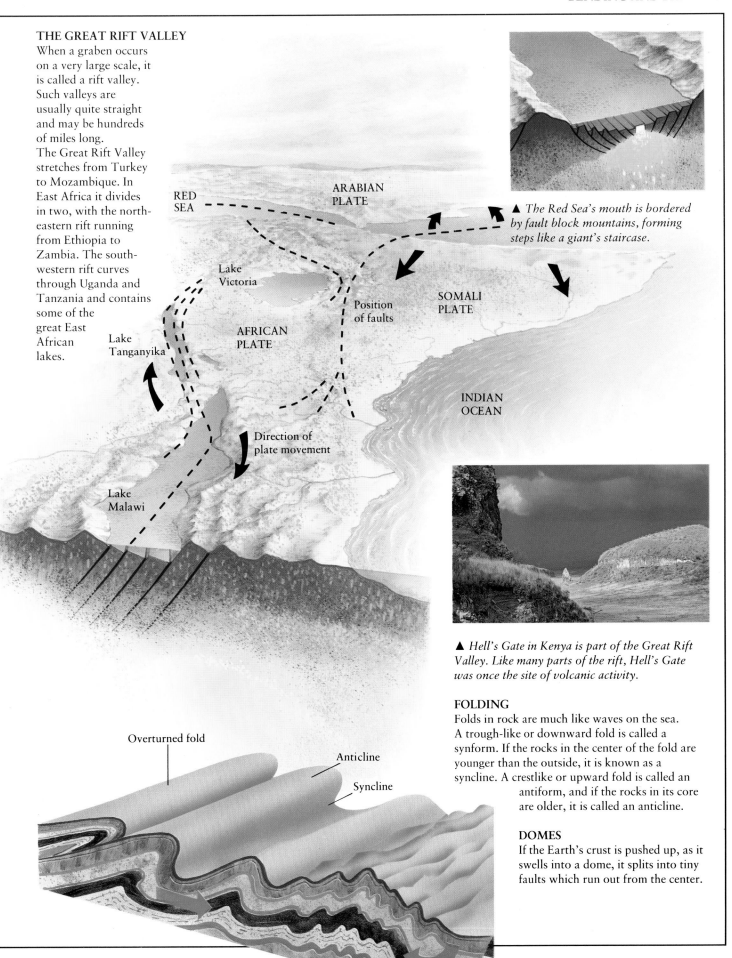

THE GREAT RIFT VALLEY

When a graben occurs on a very large scale, it is called a rift valley. Such valleys are usually quite straight and may be hundreds of miles long. The Great Rift Valley stretches from Turkey to Mozambique. In East Africa it divides in two, with the north-eastern rift running from Ethiopia to Zambia. The south-western rift curves through Uganda and Tanzania and contains some of the great East African lakes.

RED SEA

ARABIAN PLATE

Lake Victoria

Position of faults

SOMALI PLATE

AFRICAN PLATE

Lake Tanganyika

INDIAN OCEAN

Direction of plate movement

Lake Malawi

▲ *The Red Sea's mouth is bordered by fault block mountains, forming steps like a giant's staircase.*

▲ *Hell's Gate in Kenya is part of the Great Rift Valley. Like many parts of the rift, Hell's Gate was once the site of volcanic activity.*

FOLDING

Folds in rock are much like waves on the sea. A trough-like or downward fold is called a synform. If the rocks in the center of the fold are younger than the outside, it is known as a syncline. A crestlike or upward fold is called an antiform, and if the rocks in its core are older, it is called an anticline.

DOMES

If the Earth's crust is pushed up, as it swells into a dome, it splits into tiny faults which run out from the center.

Overturned fold

Anticline

Syncline

Rocks

Granite, sandstone, chalk, marble, and slate are all different types of rock. The pebbles you find on the beach are rocks that have been worn down and smoothed by the action of the sea. The stones that are used to build structures, from small cottages to magnificent cathedrals, are rocks. Not all rocks are hard; clay is a type of rock, but it is quite soft. Petrologists (scientists who study rocks) might define a rock as any natural mass of mineral matter that makes up the Earth's crust.

HOW ROCKS ARE FORMED

There are three main groups of rocks. Igneous rocks are formed from lava hurled out of a volcano, or from hot magma forced up through the ground. Sedimentary rocks are made from sediments formed by the erosion and weathering of other rocks. The sediments are carried by wind or water to the sea, where they are deposited and harden to rock. Metamorphic rocks are rocks that have been changed by heat and/or pressure.

IGNEOUS ROCKS

Granite is coarse-grained because it has cooled slowly. Syenite is similar to granite but less common. Basalt is almost black, fine-grained, and has cooled quickly.

Granite

Basalt

Syenite

Sedimentary rocks

Limestone

SEDIMENTARY ROCKS

Sandstone is made from grains of sand that have been naturally cemented together. The red rock of Devon, England, is a typical sandstone. Chalk is made up of millions of tiny calcium carbonate (lime) skeletons.

Chalk

Sandstone

GEOLOGICAL TIMESCALE

For the last 150 years, scientists have been figuring out the ages of rocks. Unless they have been overturned, the oldest rocks are deeper than younger ones. Rocks can be related to a scale of different ages.

Millions of years ago

	4600	570	505	440	410	360
Period		Precambrian	Cambrian	Ordovician	Silurian	Devonian
Era						PALEOZOIC

METAMORPHIC ROCKS

Metamorphic rocks are changed rocks. When a rock is subjected to heat and/or pressure, new minerals are formed, altering the characteristics of the rock. Slate is a hard rock formed from muds and clays. It splits easily into thin sheets.

MARBLE

Marble is a metamorphic rock. It is a type of limestone (sedimentary rock) which may have been changed by the heat of a lava flow or by contact with molten rocks far below the ground. Marble can be polished, and it may be pure white in color or mottled or banded. It has long been favored by architects and sculptors. The Carrara marble quarry in Italy *(left)* produces some of the world's finest stone.

Metamorphic rocks

Slate

Marble

Igneous rocks

285	245	210	145		65	60	35	25	5	2	0.1
Carboniferous	Permian	Triassic	Jurassic	Cretaceous		Paleocene	Eocene	Oligocene	Miocene	Pliocene	Pleistocene	Recent
								Tertiary			Quaternary
		MESOZOIC				CENOZOIC					

Minerals and Gems

Minerals are the building blocks of rocks. All rocks, igneous, sedimentary, or metamorphic, are composed of minerals. A mineral is a chemical compound that occurs naturally. Each different mineral is made up of crystals of a particular chemical. Minerals can be identified by their hardness, color, density, the way they reflect light, and the way they break. Sometimes, using a hand lens, you can even identify the shape of the individual crystals of a mineral within a rock.

ROCK-FORMING MINERALS

Rocks are made up of mineral grains. The most common minerals that make up igneous rocks include quartz, plagioclase, and olivine. Augite is found in metamorphic rocks. Dolomite makes up limestone sedimentary rocks.

Dolomite

Plagioclase

Olivine

Augite

▲ *One of the most common minerals is salt. Common salt is sodium chloride and occurs naturally in the sea. When an inland lake in a hot region evaporates, the salts are left behind as crystals, forming a salt pan, or growing to form pillars such as these, in the Dead Sea.*

HOW MINERALS ARE FORMED

All minerals are originally formed from hot magma. When the magma cools, crystals of minerals appear. These first crystals may sink in the magma so that the composition of the magma changes with depth. Thus, a sequence of minerals is formed in the rocks as the magma cools.

WHAT MINERALS ARE MADE OF

About 90 different chemical elements are found naturally in the Earth's crust. But almost 99 percent of all minerals are made of just 8 elements: oxygen, silicon, aluminum, iron, calcium, sodium, potassium, and magnesium. Some minerals, such as gold and diamond, consist of a single element. These minerals are called native elements.

▶ *In areas of volcanic activity, hot water under pressure may force its way into cracks in the rocks. The water contains dissolved minerals. The minerals may crystallize on the sides of the crack forming a* vein. *Important ore minerals (containing metals) are formed in this way.*

Open-pit mine

Layers of rock

Lighter minerals form near the top

Igneous intrusion (magma)

FACTS ABOUT MINERALS AND GEMS

- There are at least 2,000 minerals that have been named and identified. However, most rocks are made up of no more than 12 different classes of minerals—the rock-forming minerals.
- The most common element in the Earth's crust is oxygen, forming over 46 percent by weight. The second most common element is silicon at just over 27 percent by weight. Quartz is silicon dioxide. Quartz is a very common mineral.
- The largest diamond ever found was the Cullinan diamond, discovered in South Africa in 1905. It was 3,106 carats, which means it weighed more than 21 oz (600 g).
- The highest price ever paid for a diamond was more than $9 million.
- The largest cut emerald was 86,136 carats (well over 37 lb [17 kg]). It was found in Brazil and was valued in 1982 at over $1 million.

CRYSTAL SYSTEMS

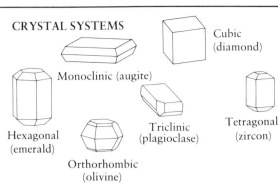

Monoclinic (augite)

Cubic (diamond)

Hexagonal (emerald)

Triclinic (plagioclase)

Tetragonal (zircon)

Orthorhombic (olivine)

▲ Many minerals form crystals. The shape of a crystal is determined by the arrangement of its atoms. A crystal has many flat faces. The angles between each face are characteristic of a given type of crystal. The whole crystal is symmetrical. On the basis of its symmetry, any crystal can be included within one of just six (sometimes seven) crystal systems.

▼ Most minerals are formed underground when heat and pressure transforms one form of rock into another. The minerals in molten rock or dissolved in very hot water crystallize out of solution as the temperature falls. Lighter minerals occur above denser minerals. If the crystals form slowly then gemstones may form.

GEMSTONES

A gemstone is a mineral that is especially beautiful and rare. Gems are formed under particular conditions of temperature and pressure, when the right minerals are present and crystals can form. These conditions are found deep in the Earth's crust. A gem may have a beautiful color: deep green emeralds or brilliant red rubies. Or its surface may show a rainbow of colors when it is moved, as in the case of opal.

Silver

Gold

▲ Gold and silver are elements. Diamond and graphite are both forms of carbon but their atoms are arranged differently. Diamond is the hardest known naturally occurring substance. It may occur as gem-quality stones. Graphite is soft, black, and feels greasy.

Diamond

Graphite

▼ Under the sea, minerals dissolved in water crystallize around the vents of faults or fissures in the Earth's crust. They also precipitate (become solid) in the sea water above the sea floor.

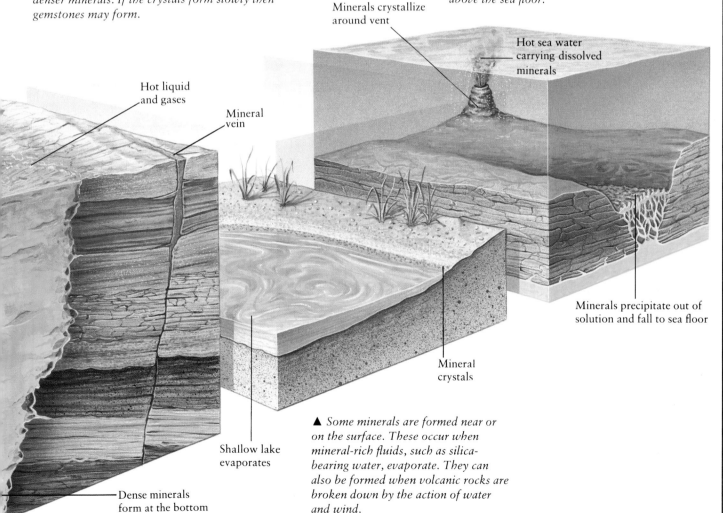

Minerals crystallize around vent

Hot sea water carrying dissolved minerals

Hot liquid and gases

Mineral vein

Minerals precipitate out of solution and fall to sea floor

Mineral crystals

Shallow lake evaporates

Dense minerals form at the bottom

▲ Some minerals are formed near or on the surface. These occur when mineral-rich fluids, such as silica-bearing water, evaporate. They can also be formed when volcanic rocks are broken down by the action of water and wind.

Frozen in Time

The word fossil comes from the Latin, *fossilis*, meaning "dug up." Until the beginning of the 18th century, fossil meant anything that was dug out of the ground. Now we use the word to describe any remains of animals or plants that lived before about 10,000 years ago. The term is also used to describe the "fossil fuels"—coal, oil, and gas—because these fuels have been formed from the remains of ancient plants and animals. Fossils include skeletons, teeth, tracks, leaves, and even plant pollen.

HOW FOSSILS ARE FORMED

Most fossils are found in sedimentary rocks, such as limestone or shale, which have been formed in the sea. Fossils of sea creatures are therefore much more common than those of land creatures. Those land animals and plants that have been preserved are usually found in sediments in a lake, river, or estuary.

The soft parts of an animal or plant —the flesh, or a delicate shoot— will decay more quickly than its hard parts after the creature dies. So shells, teeth, and bones are much more likely to be preserved as fossils than skin or organs. But sometimes, even an animal's last meal may be preserved as a fossil.

▼ *When sap runs down a tree trunk, it may trap an insect climbing up. The sap hardens into a golden-brown resin called amber, with the insect preserved inside it.*

Oil may seep up through the ground to form tar pits. An animal may fall into a pit and its remains be preserved. Parts of ancient plants are often preserved in coal.

Fossil insect in amber

Fossil leaf in coal

Tar pit

◀ *When a sea animal, such as an ammonite, dies, its body will sink to the seabed. If there are swift currents the shell may be swept around. The shell will quickly break up and itself become part of the sediment on the seabed.*

▶ *If the current is not very strong, the animal will settle and sediment will fall rapidly to the seabed, burying it. This protects the animal from being eaten and destroyed by scavengers. The animal's soft parts rot away leaving the shell.*

▲ *As the shell is buried under more and more sediment, the material around it hardens into rock as the individual grains become squeezed together. The shell may remain in its original form or it may be replaced with minerals such as quartz or lime.*

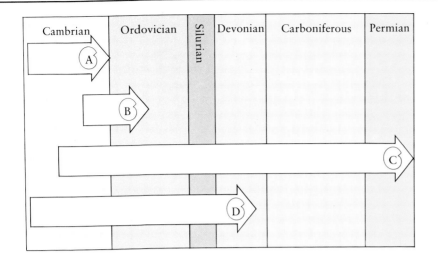

Cambrian	Ordovician	Silurian	Devonian	Carboniferous	Permian

DATING ROCKS FROM FOSSILS

Many types of animals and plants survived on Earth for only a limited period of time. Ammonites, pterosaurs, and dinosaurs all became extinct, or died out. The fossils of extinct animals can be used to date the surrounding rock. This is because these fossils cannot be found in rocks that are younger than the time at which the animal disappeared. Rocks of a known age can also be used to date fossils.

FACTS ABOUT FOSSILS

- The oldest known fossils are called stromatolites. Stromatolites are the remains of matlike structures formed by bacteria. Stromatolites have been found in western North America and Australia. Some are more than 2 billion years old.
- One of the largest fossil bones that has ever been found was the shoulder blade of a giant dinosaur called *Supersaurus*. It measured over 6.5 ft. (2 m) and was found in Colorado in 1972.
- Most of the world's fossils have been found in rocks less than 600 million years old. This is the time when animals with hard parts first evolved.
- Paleontologists (who study fossils) can learn about prehistoric climates from minute fossilized pollen grains. The pollen grains can be used as "fingerprints" to identify the plants living at particular times.

MOLDS AND CASTS

Sometimes a shell may be dissolved away by acid waters seeping through the rock. However, the shape of the shell might be preserved in the surrounding rock—a mold. If the mold is then filled with new mineral material, the resulting fossil is called a cast.

▼ *Eventually, the effects of weathering and erosion may wear away the sedimentary rocks and expose the fossil. Or the fossil may be found in a quarry face, or because of road cutting. It is as though the sea animal has been frozen in time.*

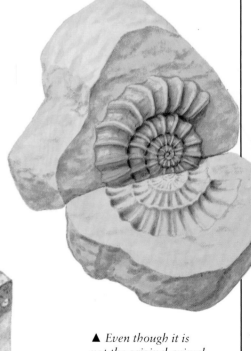

▲ *Over many millions of years, the sea may retreat. The rocks in which the fossil lies may become faulted and folded because of movements within the Earth's crust. What was once the seabed may be thrown up into a newly formed mountain range.*

▲ *Even though it is not the original animal that has been preserved, scientists can still learn a lot from the fossil.*

Shaping the Earth

The world's highest mountain is Mount Everest in the Himalaya range, soaring to 29,028 ft. (8,848 m). Britain's highest mountain, Ben Nevis, is 4,406 ft. (1,343 m). Both mountains were created by similar processes of mountain building, so why should one be nearly seven times the height of the other? Part of the answer lies in the effects of weathering and erosion. Ben Nevis is a very old mountain and has been worn down over hundreds of millions of years by the action of wind, rain, ice, and snow.

▲ *Plant roots can also break down rock. They work their way into tiny cracks in a rock. As the roots grow, they widen the cracks. Eventually, the force of the roots can shatter the rock. Worms eat large amounts of soil, passing out the waste as casts which can then be washed away by rain.*

WEATHERING AND EROSION

Rocks are often formed inside the Earth at high pressures and temperatures. At the Earth's surface, when rocks are exposed, the conditions are quite different. It is this change that causes rocks and minerals to break up. Physical weathering breaks down the rocks into smaller particles, such as sands or grits. In chemical weathering, the minerals that form the rocks are dissolved by the action of water, together with oxygen and carbon dioxide in the air. Once the rocks have been broken down by weathering, the bits are transported elsewhere by ice, wind, running water, or gravity. This is called erosion. Sometimes the actions of people, such as removing plants that hold the soil together, can increase erosion.

▼ *These desert rocks have been scoured by sand-carrying wind into strange pillars appearing from the dunes.*

▼ *Rain containing dissolved carbon dioxide from the air is a weak acid and will dissolve calcite, the main mineral found in limestones.*

Scree formed by frost erosion

Erosion of river valley

▼ *Rivers carry weathered rock debris to the coast. The finest particles may be carried out to sea.*

Erosion and weathering of folded rocks at surface

Rock tower weathered by wind and rain

▶ *When water freezes, it expands. If water finds its way into cracks in rocks and then freezes, it pushes out against the rock. This may cause the rock to shatter.*

◀ *Rocks may be subjected to high temperatures during the day, and very low ones at night. They expand and contract, which causes them to split.*

SLUMPS AND SLIDES

Gravity often causes erosion. Soil may slide slowly down a slope as a result of disturbance caused by wetting and drying. And gravity can cause loose material to slump. If the material is dry, some kind of shock, such as an earthquake, may cause soil and rock to slump.

▲ Soil may creep slowly downhill, pulled by gravity.

▲ A shock may cause clay to liquefy to form a mudflow.

▲ In a landslide, material falls quite quickly, but the material may

fall from a break along a plane or curved surface.

FACTS ABOUT CAVES AND CAVERNS

● The world's deepest cave is at Rousseau Jean Bernard, in France. It is 5,036 ft. (1,535 m) deep.
● The longest cave system in the world is at least 330 mi. (530 km) long. It is under the Mammoth Cave National Park, Kentucky.
● The world's biggest cavern is the Sarawak Chamber in Sarawak, Indonesia. It is 2,300 ft. (700 m) long, 1,000 ft. (300 m) wide, and 230 ft. (70 m) high, and is supported only by its sides.
● Gaping Gyll, a sinkhole in North Yorkshire, England, descends vertically for more than 360 ft. (110 m).
● The longest stalactite in the world is in a cavern in County Clare in Ireland. It is over 23 ft. (7 m) long.
● Near Lozère in southern France, there is a stalagmite that has now reached 95 ft. (29 m) in height.

CAVES AND CAVERNS

Limestone may be weathered into a pavement of blocks. As acid water works its way down through cracks in limestone, it widens the cracks into passageways. When the water meets a layer it cannot drain through, it runs down until it finds an exit. In this way underground streams and rivers are formed. They dissolve away the limestone to form potholes, caves, and caverns.

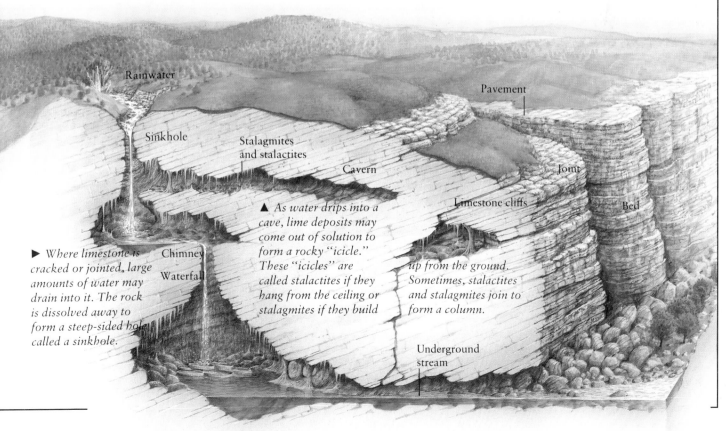

Rainwater

Sinkhole

Stalagmites and stalactites

Cavern

Pavement

Joint

Limestone cliffs

Bed

► Where limestone is cracked or jointed, large amounts of water may drain into it. The rock is dissolved away to form a steep-sided hole called a sinkhole.

Chimney

Waterfall

▲ As water drips into a cave, lime deposits may come out of solution to form a rocky "icicle." These "icicles" are called stalactites if they hang from the ceiling or stalagmites if they build

up from the ground. Sometimes, stalactites and stalagmites join to form a column.

Underground stream

The Work of Ice

Water freezes into solid ice at 32°F (0°C). As the density of water is greatest at 39.2°F (4°C), ice floats on top of cold water. This is important because it allows animals and plants to survive below the ice on a river, lake, or even the ocean, provided the water does not freeze solid. A large block of ice that floats in the sea is called an iceberg. A large mass of ice on the surface of the land is called a glacier. Glaciers, originally made of snow, are very powerful and their action carves distinctive landscapes.

GLACIERS

Glaciers will form in places where so much snow falls during the winter that not all of it melts or evaporates in the summer. Glaciers are often found high up in mountains at the heads of valleys. Above the snow line, snow accumulates as a permanent snowfield.

ICE AGES

A period when part of the Earth is permanently covered by ice is called an Ice Age. We are living in an Ice Age at the moment. There are permanent ice sheets at the North and South poles. The extent of the ice varies with the seasons. However, there have been times in the past when larger areas of continents have been covered with ice. This was because the Earth's climate was cooler then.

☐ Present extent of ice sheet
☐ Farthest extent of ice sheet

▶ As the layers of snow build up, they pack close together under the weight of the snow above. Dense snow is called névé.

▶ Air is squeezed out of the névé while water runs into it and freezes. The névé becomes denser.

Depth (ft.)	
	Fresh snow
0	
3	Névé
	Compacted snow
30	
	Ice
80	
150	
300	Compressed glacier ice
	Impermeable ice
600	

▲ Eventually the white snow is turned into clear, bluish ice, forming a glacier.

Ice Age

60°
50°
40°
32°

Average July temperatures (°F)

200,000   160,000   140,000   80,000   40,000   20,000   8   4   Present

Years before present

GLACIATION

About 2 million years ago, the Earth's climate cooled and polar ice spread southward, covering Europe as far south as the Severn Estuary in Britain. In places, the European ice sheet was as thick as the Greenland ice sheet is today. The results of glaciation can be seen today. Valleys contained huge glaciers, creeping slowly downhill. As a glacier moved its scouring action wore away the sides and floor of its valley, deepening it. Glaciated valleys can be recognized by their smooth U-shape. And because ice does not meander as the river did, the valley is straightened out and old spurs (projections) cut off.

▼ A glacier carries with it rock debris from its valley. As the snout of the glacier melts, some debris is dropped, forming a ridge called a terminal moraine.

Meltwater

Snout

Terminal moraine

FACTS ABOUT ICE

- Today, permanent ice covers more than 10 percent of the Earth's surface.
- During the last Ice Age, over 28 percent of the planet was engulfed in ice. The Scandinavian ice sheet was 10,000 ft. (3,000 m) thick.
- During the Ice Ages, the average temperature of the Earth was only about 5°F (3°C) lower than it is today.
- The world's longest glacier is the Antarctic Lambert Glacier which is over 250 mi. (400 km) in length.
- The fastest moving glacier, in Greenland, flows at up to 79 ft. (24 m) a day.
- The greatest thickness of ice is in the Antarctic and is about 16,400 ft. (5,000 m).
- The biggest iceberg ever sighted was more than 12,000 sq. mi. (31,000 sq. km) in size.

▼ *The head of a glaciated valley is weathered and eroded into an armchair-shape known as a cirque. Where more than one cirque is linked, a knifelike ridge or a pyramid-shaped peak may result.*

Pyramidal peak

Cirque

► *A typical river valley is a V shape. A moving glacier carries a great deal of rock with it. It works muck like sandpaper, wearing away at the valley until its shape is like a U.*

Crevasses

Movement of glacier

Lateral moraine

► *Sometimes a glacier picks up large blocks of rock and dumps them a long distance away. These are called glacial erratics.*

◄ *Lakes may form in the armchair-shaped cirques made by glaciers.*

GLACIAL LAKES

Lakes are a common feature of a landscape that has been glaciated. Indeed, there are more glacial lakes than all other kinds put together. A lake may form in a hollow that the ice has worn in softer rocks, or in holes in the uneven surface where a glacier has deposited a lot of debris.

WATER

Oceans and Seas

Over 70 percent of the Earth's surface is covered by water—the rivers, lakes, oceans, and seas. This watery layer is sometimes referred to as the hydrosphere. There is also water locked up as ice—mainly at the poles—and still more exists as vapor in the atmosphere and as moisture in the soil. But about 97 percent of the planet's water is in the seas, and it is salty. The oceans are not evenly distributed around the globe, and most of the world's land areas are to be found in the Northern Hemisphere. The world's biggest ocean is the Pacific. It occupies almost twice the area of the next biggest ocean, the Atlantic, and is also far deeper. Much of the Pacific coast is bounded by mountain ranges, such as the Andes. This means that there are few major rivers flowing into the Pacific Ocean. Many large rivers flow into the Atlantic, carrying sediment from the land.

BEYOND THE LAND

The ocean floor can be separated into two main zones: the deep ocean basin, and the shallower area at the edge of the land, called the continental margin. The gentle slope from the edge of the land down to about 1,600 ft. (500 m) is the continental shelf. Farther out to sea, the ocean bed falls away more steeply down the continental slope, between 5,000 and 11,500 ft. (1,500–3,500 m) to the abyssal plain. Deep submarine canyons form in the continental slope, where currents of muddy water from the mouths of rivers rush down the slope and deposit their sediments in a fan shape.

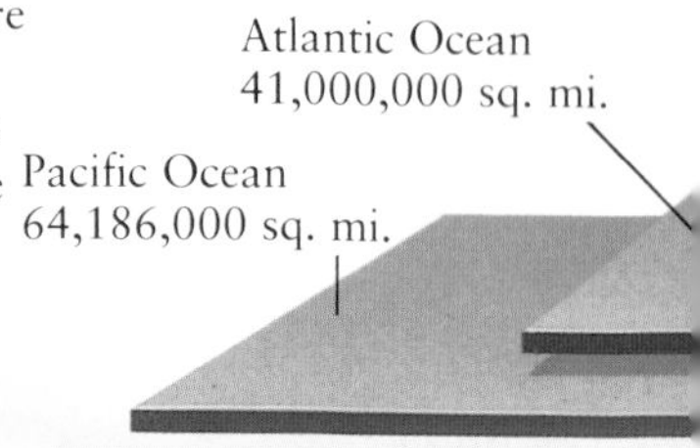

Atlantic Ocean
41,000,000 sq. mi.

Pacific Ocean
64,186,000 sq. mi.

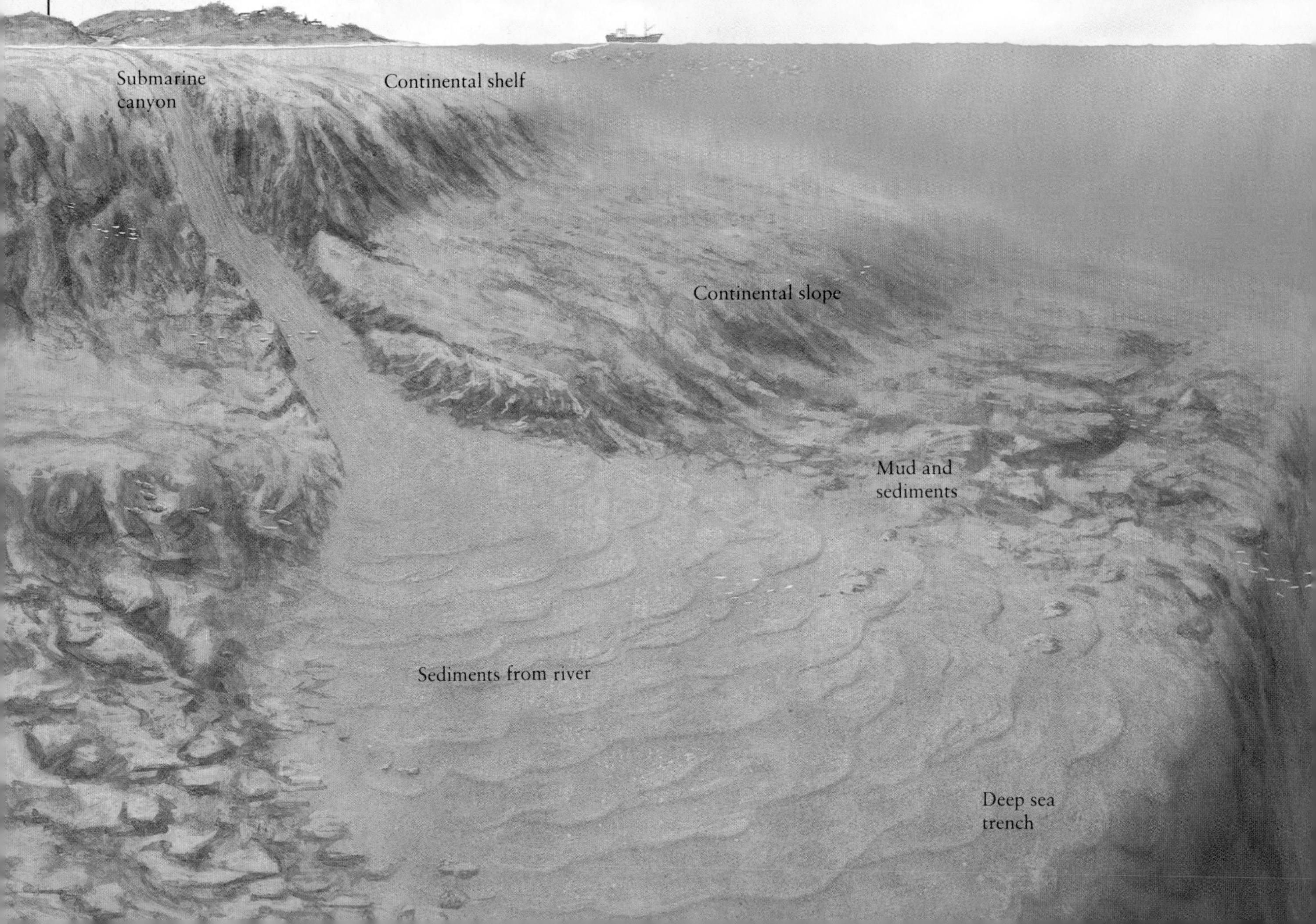

Submarine canyon

Continental shelf

Continental slope

Mud and sediments

Sediments from river

Deep sea trench

THE OCEANS

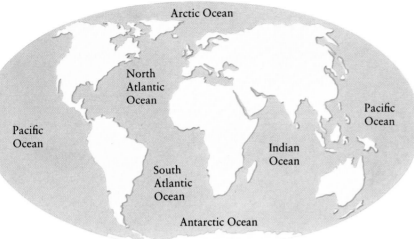

Arctic Ocean

North Atlantic Ocean

Pacific Ocean

Pacific Ocean

Indian Ocean

South Atlantic Ocean

Antarctic Ocean

Indian Ocean 28,380,000 sq. mi.

Antarctic Ocean 12,450,000 sq. mi.

Arctic Ocean 5,540,000 sq. mi.

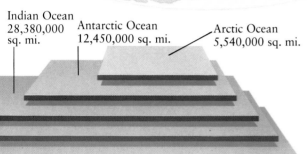

◄ *Two-thirds of the world's surface is covered by the oceans and seas. Of the five oceans, the Pacific is by far the largest.*

FACTS ABOUT OCEANS AND SEAS

- The total area of the oceans is about 140 million sq. mi. (362 million sq. km).
- The Pacific Ocean is about 64 million sq. mi. (166 million sq. km) in area.
- The deepest part of the ocean is the Marianas Trench, in the Pacific Ocean. It is 36,198 ft. (11,033 m) deep.
- The tallest seamount under the ocean is situated between Samoa and New Zealand and is 28,510 ft. (8,690 m) high.
- The largest sea is the South China Sea with an area of 1,148,500 sq. mi. (2,974,600 sq. km).
- Hudson Bay is the world's biggest bay and has an area of 475,000 sq. mi. (1,230,250 sq. km).
- Most of the ocean floors are covered by a layer of loose sediments up to 0.6 mi. (1 km) thick.

CORAL REEFS AND ATOLLS

Corals are sea animals related to jellyfish. An individual, known as a polyp, has a cylinder-like trunk which is fixed at one end and has a mouth at the other. Some corals live in vast colonies and build massive limey skeletons which accumulate into reefs.

MOUNTAINS AND CANYONS

The mountains of the oceans are very tall indeed. Mauna Kea, Hawaii, is really the peak of a mountain that starts on the sea bottom. Measured from there it is taller than Everest. Similarly, the Grand Canyon is dwarfed by the Marianas Trench in the Pacific Ocean. A volcanic mountain under the sea is called a seamount. If it breaks the surface, it becomes an island. Its top may be eroded and flat so it no longer breaks the sea surface. Then it is known as a guyot.

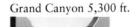

Mount Everest 29,028 ft.

Mauna Kea 33,480 ft.

Grand Canyon 5,300 ft.

Marianas Trench 36,000 ft.

◄ *Close to mid-ocean ridges, there are holes in the seafloor where hot liquids and gases leak into the water from the hot rocks beneath. These liquids include metal oxides and sulfides which give a smokelike effect as they mix with the cold seawater. Some animals live near these "smokers," feeding on the sulfides.*

◄ *Coral reefs form when a new volcanic island rises from the sea over a hot spot. A fringing coral reef grows up around the island.*

◄ *The coral grows as fast as the seafloor sinks, or the sea level rises. This makes a barrier reef with a lagoon between it and the island.*

◄ *Eventually the island disappears, leaving an atoll enclosing an empty lagoon, or a ring-shaped reef. Finally the coral is also covered by the rising waters, or sinks with the subsiding seabed.*

The Life of the Ocean

The world of the oceans and seas has sometimes been called "inner space." Humans have made use of the sea for thousands of years – for food, transportation, and as a waste dump, for example. However, it has been only in comparatively recent times that people have been able to use machines to explore the fascinating world beneath the surface. The sea also has a considerable effect upon the land and the life that lives there. Water heats and cools quite slowly, and the oceans moderate the world's climate.

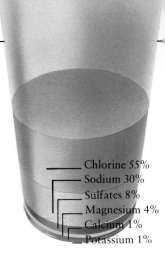

▶ *The sea tastes salty because it contains common salt and other minerals. On average, the salinity of the sea is 35 parts per thousand. Some inland lakes and seas are saltier than the oceans —the Dead Sea is 250 parts per thousand.*

Chlorine 55%
Sodium 30%
Sulfates 8%
Magnesium 4%
Calcium 1%
Potassium 1%

OCEAN CURRENTS

Warm water is less dense than, and rises through, colder water. In the deep waters of the oceans, these differences in temperature and density create currents. In the top 1,600 ft. (500 m) of water, it is the winds that drive the currents. The ocean's currents follow the prevailing wind directions. Therefore in each ocean basin, there is a roughly circular movement of water called a gyre.

➡ Warm water
➡ Cold water

▼ *Near the equator, the ocean's main currents are blown toward the west. Near the poles, they are blown eastward.*

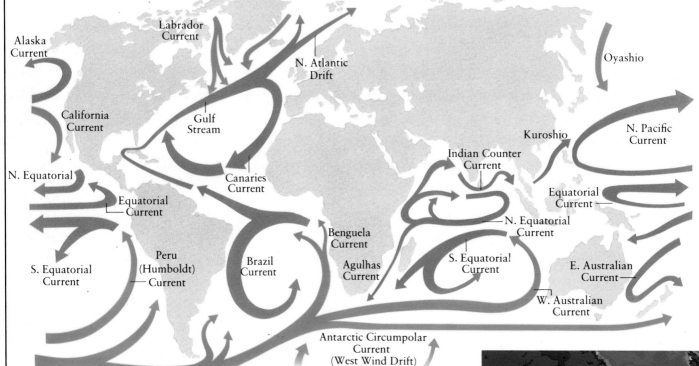

Labrador Current

Alaska Current

N. Atlantic Drift

Oyashio

California Current

Gulf Stream

Kuroshio

N. Pacific Current

N. Equatorial

Canaries Current

Indian Counter Current

Equatorial Current

Equatorial Current

N. Equatorial Current

Benguela Current

S. Equatorial Current

E. Australian Current

S. Equatorial Current

Peru (Humboldt) Current

Brazil Current

Agulhas Current

W. Australian Current

Antarctic Circumpolar Current (West Wind Drift)

Antarctic Circumpolar Current (West Wind Drift)

▶ *In 1947, the Norwegian scientist Thor Heyerdahl built a balsawood raft—the Kon-Tiki. The raft was named after an ancient Peruvian. According to legend, this Peruvian had floated from Peru across the Pacific Ocean to settle in the Polynesian Islands. Heyerdahl's raft did reach the islands. Both the Peruvians and Heyerdahl were probably helped on their way by the Humboldt Current.*

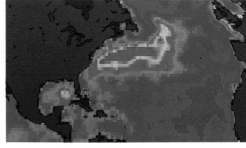

▲ *The Gulf Stream is a current of warm water that begins in the Gulf of Mexico, runs up the coast of the eastern United States, and then turns eastward across the Atlantic toward Europe.*

THE THERMOCLINE

The waters of the top 328 ft. (100 m) of the seas are mixed by the wind. Beneath this, the water temperature falls rapidly. The boundary between the two levels is the thermocline. It prevents nutrients in the water from moving upward.

Depth (miles)

Thermocline

0.5

1.25

2.0

2.5

► *Sunlight penetrates water to about 3,000 ft. (900 m) but only the top 328 ft. (100 m) gets enough light for plants to photosynthesize. Seaweeds that live in upper waters are green and those below are reddish.*

LIFE IN THE SEA

The sea provides support and food for countless animals and plants. Although some kinds of sea creatures may exist in vast numbers, less than 15 percent of the world's species of animals live in the oceans. And 98 percent of these dwell on the seafloor.

Plankton

Small fish

Sharks

Squid

◄ *Below 3,000 ft. (900 m) the oceans are pitch black. At depths greater than 6,500 ft. (2,000 m), strange creatures survive. Some of them give out their own light signals. Beardworms and fish called rat-tails live here, but there may be other even weirder animals that scientists have yet to discover.*

Angler fish

Deep sea shrimp

BROTHER AND SISTER

El Niño (the Spanish word for a boy) is the name given to an occasional change in the world's weather pattern. This change, in turn, affects the circulation of the world's oceans.

Normal Conditions

PACIFIC OCEAN

Australia

Warm water

South America

Cold water

El Niño

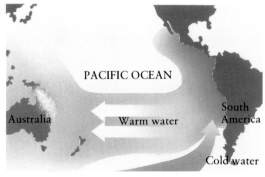

PACIFIC OCEAN

Australia

Warm water

South America

◄ *Usually, food-rich waters well up along the coast of Peru, but during El Niño the winds change and the upwelling of cold, rich water is stopped. Instead, warm water arrives at the coast killing much of the wildlife and bringing famine to the people. La Niña (the Spanish for a girl) is the name given to a second occasional weather pattern which has the opposite effect to El Niño. When it occurs, it brings drought to some parts of the world while others are subjected to freak rains and floods.*

THE SARGASSO SEA

As ocean currents circulate, they sometimes trap areas of relatively calm water. The Sargasso in the western North Atlantic is surrounded by the Florida Current. It is often windless and is choked with seaweed. It is the birthplace of common eels.

The Seashore

Many scientists are worried that, if the greenhouse effect (*see page 79*) continues, there will be a warming of the Earth's climate. If they are correct, then some of the polar ice would melt and sea levels across the world would rise. This could be disastrous for low-lying coastal regions. But it has happened before, about 10,000 to 15,000 years ago, toward the end of the last Ice Age. The effect continued until only a few thousand years ago. So most of the world's coasts are quite young features.

THE POWER OF THE SEA

Even the everyday action of a relatively calm sea may erode a coastline. Waves, armed with rocks, will hammer their load against the shore. And the sea will pick up and carry off any loose debris. The back-and-forth motion of rocks can smooth and round them into pebbles. Where the sea comes into contact with limestones, it may actually dissolve away the rock.

THE CHANGING COASTS

There are different types of coastline: narrow, pebbly, or sandy beaches with a steep cliff at the back; broad beaches which slope down to the sea; or rocky shores. The coast may be cut by bays or deep inlets called fjords. Where parts of the coast are being eroded by the sea, you will see bays and high cliffs. This high coast is said to be retreating before the advance of the sea. At a retreating coastline the beach helps to resist the power of the sea. The sea also builds up parts of the coast. Waves carry sand and pebbles, which are deposited in some places, building up a marsh, a beach, or a spit. This creates a low, sloping coastline.

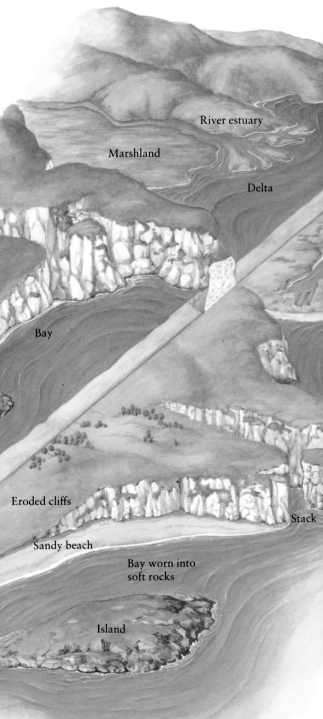

River estuary

Marshland

Delta

Bay

Eroded cliffs

Stack

Sandy beach

Bay worn into soft rocks

Island

▼ *The seashore is constantly changing. Where coastal rocks are soft the features change quickly, but where the rocks are hard, they erode slowly. A shore may feature cliffs, wide bays, rocky headlands, river deltas, and estuaries.*

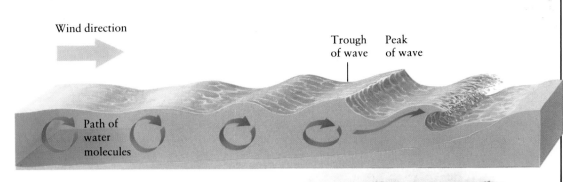

Wind direction

Trough of wave   Peak of wave

Path of water molecules

▲ *Waves are caused mainly by the wind. A wave's height depends on the strength of the wind and the area of sea it is blowing over. The motion of a water particle is almost circular until the wave meets the slope of the beach.*

SHIFTING SANDS

When a wave breaks on a beach the uprush of water (swash) carries sand and pebbles toward the land. The returning backwash takes some material back down the beach.

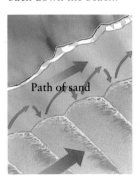

Path of sand

Longshore current

Spit

▲ *Waves may hit the beach at an angle, and a longshore current carries sand along the shore.*

◄ *The steep-sided inlets along the coast of countries such as Norway, Scotland, and New Zealand are called fjords. They are the remains of glaciated river valleys that have been flooded at a retreating coastline.*

SPITS AND BARS

Sometimes, fence-like barriers are used to prevent longshore currents from carrying beach material along the shore. But where longshore drift occurs, the sand and pebbles can be dropped into deeper water. This builds up to form a new area of land called a spit, which will continue to grow (*left*). Sand dunes and marshes often build up behind the spit. Sometimes a spit will grow right across a bay to form a bar.

Lagoon

Bar

Arch

▲ *After years of battering, the seashore may feature wide, sandy beaches where the rock was soft; an island where a headland has been cut off from the shore; stacks and arches where weaknesses in the cliffs have been worn away; and a spit at the mouth of a bay.*

FACTS ABOUT THE SEASHORE

● During a big storm, a wave can crash against the shore with a pressure of almost 66,000 pounds per square yard!

● After an Ice Age, when the ice sheets melt and their weight is removed from the land, the land may rise slowly, like a bobbing cork on water. At the coastline, the original beach will be raised high and dry and a new beach is formed at sea level.

▲ *The sea may sweep away more than the beach. Villages on a clay cliff in Yorkshire, England, have been undercut, and the erosion is still continuing.*

Rivers

Although rivers make up only a tiny percentage of all the surface water on Earth, they are very important. They wear away and form the landscape around us. River valleys have been barriers to the movement of people. Rivers themselves have provided vital transportation links from the sea to inland areas. Where bridges have been built to cross rivers, villages, towns, and cities have grown up. And of course, rivers have supplied food, and water for drinking, washing, and irrigation.

BIRTH AND DEATH OF A RIVER

Some rivers start life as springs. Others are fed by melting glaciers. Most rivers come from the rain and snow that fall on highlands. Water runs along the surface in small rivulets. These rivulets may join to form a small stream. This stream will then begin to erode a valley. The valley sides themselves provide slopes for other tributary streams to flow down. As the amount of water increases, the river grows bigger. At the end of its journey, the river flows to the sea.

▼ *When a landscape has been newly uplifted, the land surface is steep and irregular and the river naturally follows the pattern of the land. This is known as a consequent river.*

Glacier

Meltwater

Waterfall

Rapids

Stream

Spring

▼ *Where a river flows across hard rocks toward softer rocks, the softer rocks will be eroded. This erosion creates an abrupt increase in the slope of the river valley. As a result, the river flows more quickly and fiercely, as rapids. If the rock is eroded enough for its face to be vertical, the river will cascade over a waterfall.*

FACTS ABOUT RIVERS

• The longest river in the world is the Nile River in Africa. Running from its source in Burundi to the Mediterranean, the Nile is 4,145 mi. (6,670 km) long.
• The second longest river, the Amazon in South America, is 4,007 mi. (6,448 km). It runs from its source in the Andes Mountains of Peru to the southern Atlantic.
• The Amazon has more than 1,100 tributaries, and it carries much more water than the Nile.
• Rivers can carry amazing amounts of sediment. The Huang He (Yellow River) in China deposits rich silt over 54,690 sq. mi. (141,645 sq. km) in its flood plain and delta.

WATERFALLS
The world's longest unbroken falls of water:

Angel Falls, Venezuela 3,208 ft.
Yosemite Falls, Calif. 2,424 ft.
Mardalsfossen, Norway 2,150 ft.
Tugela, Africa 2,014 ft.

RIVER SHAPES

If a river flows quickly down a steep slope, over hard rocks, it will tend to cut a gorge, or deep cleft, in the land.

Where the river flows more slowly, over softer rocks, the valley will be worn back and widened out into an open V shape.

MEANDERS AND OXBOW LAKES

When the channel of a river flows in a snakelike pattern across the broad floor of its valley, it is said to meander. On the inner side of each curve, the river deposits sand and silt. On the outer bend, the bank is eroded away and the channel deepens. Gradually new land is built up on the inner side of the bend, and more land is eroded away on the outer side. This makes the course of the river migrate, or move, into an increasingly wide meander. As the bends migrate, the valley gradually widens and flattens. If a flood occurs, the river may cross the neck of the loop, cutting off the old channel and forming an oxbow lake.

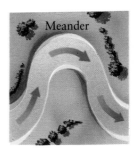

▲ *Some meanders will swell out into much broader loops than others.*

▲ *The neck of the loop may become very narrow as the loop develops.*

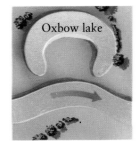

▲ *The old channel may be cut off to form an area of water called an oxbow lake.*

Tributary stream

River

Oxbow lake

Meander

Flood plain

Estuary

River mouth

▲ *As the river moves farther away from its source, its valley becomes shallower and smoother. The slope of the valley floor decreases, until it is almost flat. The river valley is broader.*

▶ *As the river reaches its mouth it slows down, dropping the sediments it has been carrying. Its valley is wide, sloping gently to the sea. The river may meander, breaking up into a number of channels.*

Lakes and Swamps

A lake is an area of water completely surrounded by land. Lakes may contain fresh or salt water. Some, such as the Caspian, the salt lake between southeastern Europe and Asia, are big enough to be thought of as inland seas. The water in a lake may seep from its basin, and it may also evaporate. So, for a lake to continue to exist, it must be fed with water at the same rate or faster than the water is being lost. And the lake's bed must be lower than the lowest part of the rim or the water will run off elsewhere.

THE LARGEST OR DEEPEST LAKE

There are two main ways that a lake can be measured. The first is the area of its surface and the second is its depth. Lake Baikal in central Siberia, Russia, is the deepest lake in the world. At its deepest point, the Olkhon Crevice, Lake Baikal is 6,365 ft. (1,940 m) deep, and 4,872 ft. (1,485 m) below sea level. The Great Lakes in North America are all linked and so could qualify as the largest by surface area.

STILL WATERS

Even though lakes seem still, few are completely stagnant. Water is at its densest at 39.2°F (4°C). So in a cold winter, the lake may be covered with a sheet of ice, while the water at the bottom of the lake is warmer. In spring, the ice melts. As the temperature of the surface water rises, it becomes denser and sinks. The water in the lake circulates until, once again, water at 39.2°F (4°C) settles to the bottom. In summer, the surface waters warm and circulate but stay above the layer of cold water in the lower part of the lake. In autumn the lake's surface cools again and the water circulates once more.

▼ *The five Great Lakes lie on the border of the United States and Canada. They are: Superior, Michigan, Huron, Erie, Ontario.*

Lake Superior

Lake Huron

Lake Michigan

Lake Erie

Lake Ontario

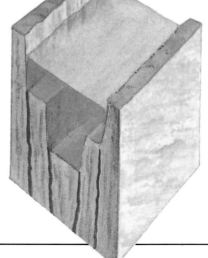

▲ *Lake Baikal is the largest freshwater lake in Eurasia, and it is the sixth biggest in the world.*

Volcanic lake

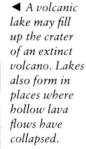

◀ *A volcanic lake may fill up the crater of an extinct volcano. Lakes also form in places where hollow lava flows have collapsed.*

Barrier lake

◀ *If a river valley becomes naturally blocked a lake will form. The barrier might be the result of a landfall, for example, or glacial debris.*

Rift valley lake

Reservoir

Dam

▶ *Sometimes people create artificial lakes. If a dam is built across a river valley, the river waters build up behind it to form a lake. Eventually this will flood the valley. The lake may be used as a reservoir to store water, or as part of a hydroelectric scheme to generate electricity.*

▶ *Lakes may lie along major fault or fissure lines, such as the long, narrow lochs in the Great Glen fault in Scotland. There are also lakes in the Great Rift Valley of East Africa—the world's largest group of fault-created lakes.*

DISAPPEARING WATERS

Most lakes are quite shallow and are fed by rivers. A river brings with it a great deal of debris and sediment. The larger particles of sediment are dropped soon after the river enters the lake, and a delta-like fan of material gradually spreads out into the water.

Very fine material may be carried quite a long way before it settles onto the lake's bed, slowly reducing the depth of water. At the same time, where the river leaves the lake, at the rim, it becomes worn away, and the lake is partly drained.

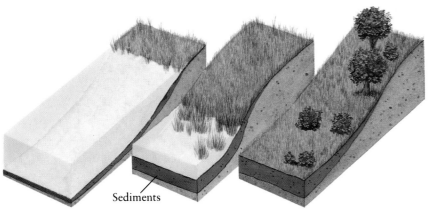

▲ A fan of sediment builds up where the river feeds the lake and deposits material.

▲ Marsh plants colonize the waterlogged soil and trap more sediment.

▲ Eventually, the land dries out and other, less marshy kinds of plants move in.

SWAMPS AND BOGS

In shallow lakes surrounded by plants, leaves and flowers fall into the water. A layer of peat-like ooze may build up. The ooze accumulates, becoming a bog or swamp.

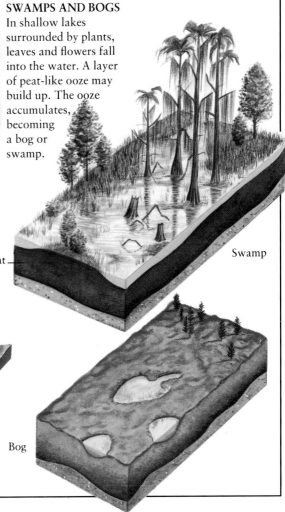

Swamp

Peat

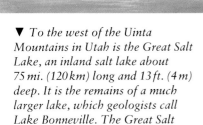

▼ To the west of the Uinta Mountains in Utah is the Great Salt Lake, an inland salt lake about 75 mi. (120 km) long and 13 ft. (4 m) deep. It is the remains of a much larger lake, which geologists call Lake Bonneville. The Great Salt Lake is getting larger without getting any less salty.

▲ The biggest inland water in the world is the Caspian Sea. It is 761 mi. (1,225 km) long. Estimates suggest that its total surface area is between 140,000 and 170,000 sq. mi. (360,000–440,000 sq. km). The Caspian is shrinking, but it is getting less salty. At its deepest point, it is about 3,280 ft. (1,000 m) deep.

Great Salt Lake

Extent of Lake Bonneville

Bog

WEATHER AND CLIMATE

The Atmosphere

The atmosphere is the envelope of air that surrounds the Earth. It has four layers: the lowest layer is the troposphere; above this layer are the stratosphere, the mesosphere, and lastly the thermosphere. The atmosphere extends upward to a height of about 300 mi. (500 km). Above this, the air merges with the particles streaming constantly from the Sun. There is no clear boundary where the Earth's atmosphere ends and that of the Sun begins. Air has weight, and the atmosphere nearest the Earth is compressed, or pressed down by the weight of the air above it. At sea level, the atmosphere presses down on every square inch of the Earth's surface with a weight of about 14.7 pounds. This pressure is called "one bar," or 1,000 millibars (mb). Atmospheric pressure decreases with height, until it falls to about one millibar at a height of 19 mi. (30 km) above sea level.

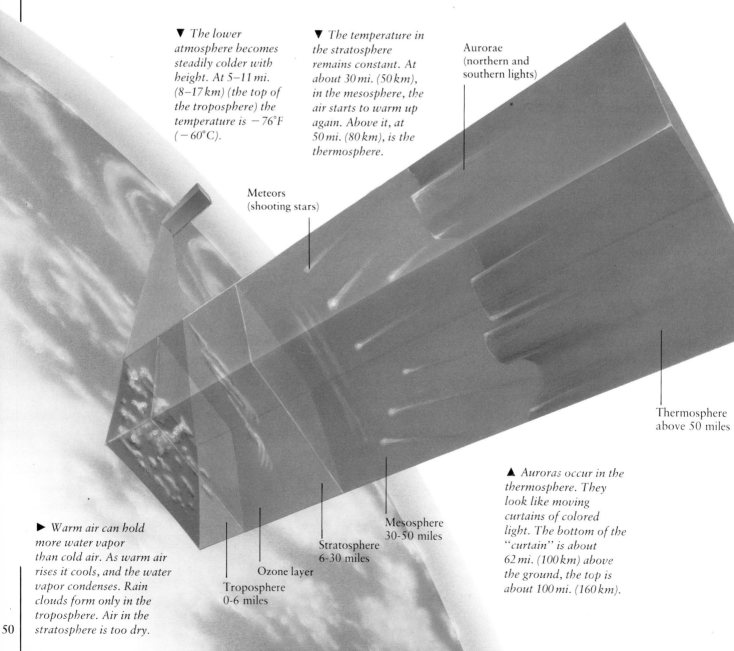

▼ *The lower atmosphere becomes steadily colder with height. At 5–11 mi. (8–17 km) (the top of the troposphere) the temperature is −76°F (−60°C).*

▼ *The temperature in the stratosphere remains constant. At about 30 mi. (50 km), in the mesosphere, the air starts to warm up again. Above it, at 50 mi. (80 km), is the thermosphere.*

Aurorae (northern and southern lights)

Meteors (shooting stars)

Thermosphere above 50 miles

Mesosphere 30-50 miles

Stratosphere 6-30 miles

Ozone layer

Troposphere 0-6 miles

▶ *Warm air can hold more water vapor than cold air. As warm air rises it cools, and the water vapor condenses. Rain clouds form only in the troposphere. Air in the stratosphere is too dry.*

▲ *Auroras occur in the thermosphere. They look like moving curtains of colored light. The bottom of the "curtain" is about 62 mi. (100 km) above the ground, the top is about 100 mi. (160 km).*

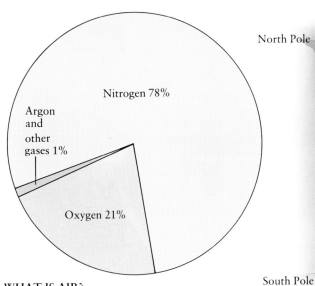

Nitrogen 78%

Argon and other gases 1%

Oxygen 21%

North Pole

Rays hit Earth at an angle

Rays hit Earth directly

South Pole

THE SUN'S RAYS

As the surface of the Earth is heated by the Sun it warms the air above it. This makes the air less dense and it rises and cools. The air over the equator is heated more strongly than over the poles, since the poles are slightly turned away from the Sun. This difference in temperature produces our climates and weather.

WHAT IS AIR?

The air is a mixture of gases: about 78 percent is nitrogen, 21 percent oxygen, and the rest is mainly argon and carbon dioxide. The air also contains water vapor, but the amount varies.

Nitrogen

| 4 billion years ago | 3.5 billion years ago | 2 billion years ago | 500 million years ago | Today |

Oxygen

Carbon dioxide

▲ *The atmosphere was once mainly carbon dioxide. By 600 million years ago, plants had replaced the carbon dioxide with oxygen, through photosynthesis. The amount of nitrogen increased until it was almost 80 percent of the air.*

CLOUDS OF THE UPPER ATMOSPHERE

Noctilucent clouds form at about 50 mi. (80 km). They are visible only on summer nights and are believed to be made up of ice crystals. Nacreous, or "mother-of-pearl," clouds form at about 14 mi. (22 km), and are visible when the Sun is just below the horizon.

Noctilucent clouds

Nacreous clouds

▲ *A view of the Moon setting over the Earth's horizon taken from space. The image of the Moon is distorted by the Earth's atmosphere.*

THE IONOSPHERE

Some radio signals are transmitted long distances by bouncing them off the ionosphere. This extends from about 62–186 mi. (100–300 km). Electrically charged air in the ionosphere reflects some radio waves.

Ionosphere

Radio waves

Earth's surface

Climate

The Sun warms the surface of the Earth more strongly near the equator than at the poles. The warm, tropical air rises and cooler, denser air from higher latitudes moves in to replace it. Water evaporates into the warm air and condenses in cool air. This constant movement of the air, driven by the warmth of the Sun, produces the world's climates and the weather we experience from day to day. It is called the "general circulation" of the atmosphere. It is influenced by the rotation of the Earth and the oceans.

GLOBAL WINDS

Warm air rises and moves away from the equator, cooling and losing moisture as it does so. The trade winds bring cold air in from higher latitudes to replace it. The dry tropical air eventually sinks in the subtropics (about 30° latitude). When it reaches the surface, some of the sinking air is drawn back to the equator, forming the trade winds, and some blows toward the poles. This circulation of the air near the equator is called the Hadley cell. It is named after George Hadley, the meteorologist who described it in 1735.

WORLD CLIMATES

The world can be divided into several climate zones. The main factors that affect the climate of a particular place are its distance from the equator (latitude) and its distance from the ocean. Climates are cooler farther away from the equator, and drier in places far from the ocean.

- Mountain
- Tropical wet and dry
- Tropical wet
- Desert
- Subtropical dry summer
- Continental moist
- Oceanic moist
- Subarctic
- Polar

JET STREAMS

There is a sharp change in temperature between warm tropical air and the cooler air north and south of the tropics, and between this mid-latitude air and polar air. In these two regions, at about 7 mi. (12 km), westerly winds blow at speeds of about 125 mph (200 km/h). These fast-moving winds are called jet streams.

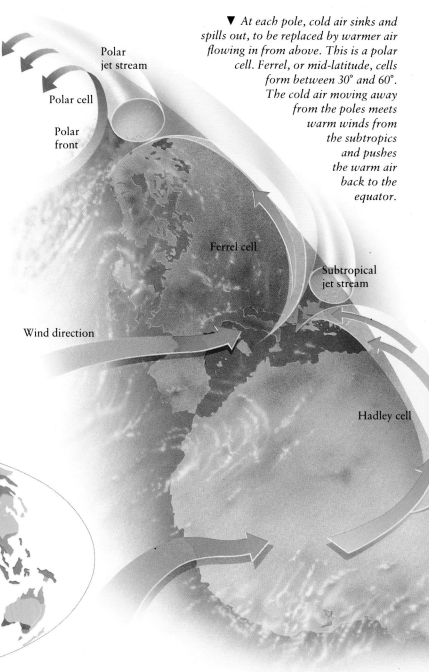

▼ At each pole, cold air sinks and spills out, to be replaced by warmer air flowing in from above. This is a polar cell. Ferrel, or mid-latitude, cells form between 30° and 60°. The cold air moving away from the poles meets warm winds from the subtropics and pushes the warm air back to the equator.

Polar jet stream

Polar cell

Polar front

Ferrel cell

Subtropical jet stream

Wind direction

Hadley cell

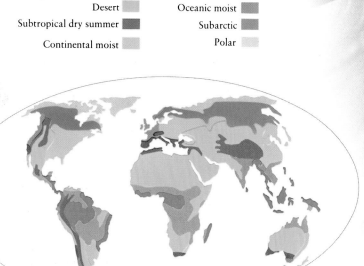

THE CORIOLIS EFFECT

The Earth rotates to the east; the surface and the air move faster at the equator. Warm air rises and is replaced by cooler air which is moving eastward more slowly, so the Earth's surface overtakes it. This creates the northeasterly and southeasterly trade winds and is called the Coriolis effect.

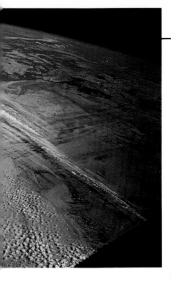

▲ *Jet streams are often revealed by long narrow bands of cirrus cloud.*

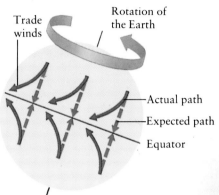

MONSOONS

In June, differences in air pressure over land and sea bring thunderstorms and heavy rain to India and southern Asia. The parched ground revives and farm crops flourish. The rainy season is called the monsoon. It lasts until September, and in some places 85 percent of the annual rain falls during this period. Monsoon seasons also occur in West Africa and northern Australia.

AIR MASSES

An air mass is a large body of air that has the same temperature and moisture. Depending on where it forms, it is called "polar" or "tropical," and "maritime" or "continental." Continental air (forming over land) is dry and cool if it is polar, and warm if it forms at the tropics. Maritime air (forming over sea) is moist. As the air mass crosses the land it loses moisture, bringing rain. The weather usually changes when one air mass is replaced by another. The boundary between two air masses is a front.

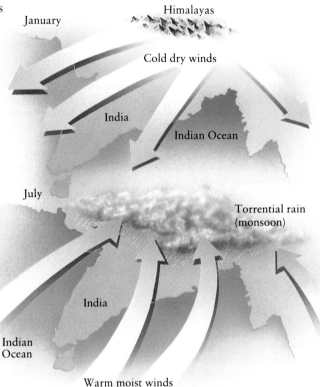

▼ *In winter, the sea is warm relative to the land. The air above the sea is heated and rises, and cold, dry winds from the northeast blow toward the Indian Ocean.*

January
Himalayas
Cold dry winds
India
Indian Ocean
July
Torrential rain (monsoon)
India
Indian Ocean
Warm moist winds

▲ *In summer, the air over northern India becomes very hot and dry. Its pressure falls, causing warm moist air to move to the north, bringing heavy rain to southern Asia.*

▲ *An area of low air pressure is called a depression. As the air rises its moisture condenses, layers of cloud form, and it rains.*

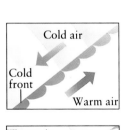

Cold air
Cold front
Warm air

◀ *A cold front has cooler and often drier air behind it.*

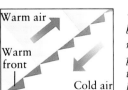

Warm air
Warm front
Cold air

◀ *A warm front brings cloud and rain. Cold air pushes beneath the warm air and lifts it.*

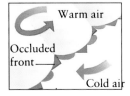

Warm air
Occluded front
Cold air

◀ *Where cold and warm air mix, the fronts are "occluded." They weaken and disappear.*

FACTS ABOUT CLIMATES

● The winds drive the ocean currents, which also carry warmth from the equator to cooler regions.

● The ocean currents affect climates by bringing warm or cool water to the shores of continents.

● The climate of western Europe is warmed by the waters of the Gulf Stream and North Atlantic Drift.

● The climate of the northwest coast of North America is cooled by the California Current, which flows south from the Arctic.

● Water warms and cools more slowly than land. A continental air mass that crosses the ocean will be warmed by the water in winter, and cooled in summer.

● The greatest amount of rain ever recorded in a single year was at Cherrapunji in India. It received 67.740 ft. (20.647 m) of rain in the monsoon season of 1861.

Winds and Storms

Air moves from areas of high atmospheric pressure to areas of low pressure, causing winds. It does not flow directly but moves around the centers of high or low pressure because of the Coriolis effect *(see page 53)*. In the Northern Hemisphere, air moves counterclockwise around low pressure and clockwise around high pressure. In the Southern Hemisphere the opposite occurs. The wind always moves "downhill" from high to low pressure. Its speed depends on the difference in pressure.

WINDS OF THE WORLD

Because the Earth spins to the east, the winds either side of the equator are from the northeast and southeast. They are the "trade winds." Between the trade wind belts lie the "doldrums," where winds are light. In middle latitudes (30°–50°), winds are more often from the west than from the east. Easterly winds prevail in the Arctic and Antarctic.

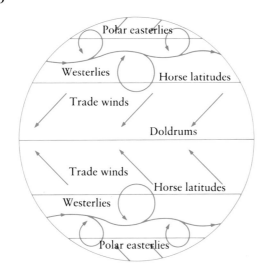

THE BEAUFORT WIND SCALE

In 1806, Sir Francis Beaufort, an English admiral, devised a scale for measuring wind force. It is still used today.

Force	Speed	Definition
0	<1 mph	calm
1	1–3 mph	light air
2	4–7 mph	light breeze
3	8–12 mph	gentle breeze
4	13–18 mph	moderate breeze
5	19–24 mph	fresh breeze
6	25–31 mph	strong breeze
7	32–38 mph	moderate gale
8	39–46 mph	fresh gale
9	47–54 mph	strong gale
10	55–63 mph	whole gale
11	64–75 mph	storm
12	>75 mph	hurricane

Wind speed is measured by an anemometer *(see page 60)*. It has small cups, mounted on horizontal arms, which spin around on an axis. A wind vane is a flat blade that indicates wind direction.

▶ *The strong upcurrents of air in heavy rainstorms have been known to lift up objects as large as fish and frogs, which then appear to rain down from the sky.*

THUNDER AND LIGHTNING

In a large storm cloud, as water droplets collide, water becomes electrically charged. Positive charges collect at the top of the cloud and negative charges at the bottom. The negative charge creates a positive charge on the ground surface, which builds until lightning sparks from the cloud to the ground and back again.

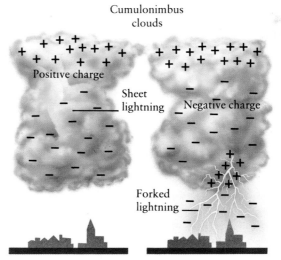

Cumulonimbus clouds

Positive charge

Sheet lightning

Negative charge

Forked lightning

▲ *Sheet lightning flashes inside or between clouds; forked lightning flashes to the ground. Thunder is the sound of hot air exploding.*

FACTS ABOUT WIND

- A warm, dry "föhn" or "chinook" wind is caused by air flowing down the side of a mountain range.
- In southern Europe, the valleys of the Rhône and other rivers funnel the "mistral," a cold, northerly wind.
- In West Africa, a dry easterly wind is called the "harmattan," or "doctor," because it brings relief from very humid conditions.
- Winds on Mt. Washington, New Hampshire, have reached 231 mph (370 km/h).

TORNADOES
A tornado is a twisting funnel, a thousand feet across, in which wind speeds can reach 220 mph (350 km/h). Tornadoes move in a straight line and can cause terrible destruction. The pressure inside is so low that it can cause nearby buildings to explode.

▶ A hurricane is a tropical storm, usually about 400 mi. (650 km) across. It brings heavy rain and winds of up to 125 mph (200 km/h). In the northwest Pacific they are called typhoons, and those in the Indian Ocean and north of Australia are called cyclones.

▶ Hurricanes form in late summer and fall over warm water in the Atlantic, Pacific, and Indian oceans. They then move westward, along coasts.

Typhoons Apr.–Dec.

Cyclones Dec.–Apr.

Hurricanes Aug.–Oct.

Hurricanes June–Oct.

Cyclones May–Dec.

Direction of storm

Eye

Dry air sinks

Strong spiral winds

Strong upcurrents

Cumulonimbus clouds

Warm moist air

Low pressure at core

Inward flowing winds

Prevailing wind direction

Warm sea

Rain

INSIDE A HURRICANE
In the eye of a hurricane, winds are light and the sky is clear. The descending air is warm and the pressure is very low. Fierce winds bring air swirling around the eye. The air is swept upward by huge cumulonimbus clouds. As air in the clouds rises and cools, the water vapor it carries condenses. This releases heat, which warms the air again, sending it upward into a region of high pressure above the clouds. The big clouds cause heavy rain. Away from the center, cirrus and cirrostratus clouds trace the storm's outline.

The Types of Cloud

Clouds form when water vapor condenses into tiny droplets. The conditions under which this happens vary, producing clouds of different types and shapes. White puffy clouds are often seen on fine days. If they grow bigger, rain showers may fall from them. High above them, there may be small wispy clouds made from ice crystals. Very large dark clouds bring thunderstorms. Layers of cloud, like flat sheets covering the sky, bring dull weather or steady, sometimes heavy, rain.

CLOUD FORMATIONS
A weather front slopes, as warm air rises above cold air. As the front approaches, a series of cloud types appears. Each type is formed at a different height.

▲ *Cirrus, made from ice crystals, forms long, thin wisps of cloud aligned with the wind at about 40,000 ft. (12,000 m) high. Sometimes, the wisps separate at the ends, to form "mare's tails."*

▲ *Cirrocumulus is a thin, puffy cloud, often in ripples, made from ice crystals. It forms at about 30,000 ft. (9,000 m).*

◄ *Cirrostratus, made from ice crystals, is a thin sheet of cloud which forms at heights above 20,000 ft. (6,000 m). It often forms a halo around the Sun.*

▼ *Cumulonimbus is a dark storm cloud, with rain. It may be 6 mi (10 km) in diameter.*

◄ *Altocumulus is a white puffy cloud that sometimes forms layers or rolls between 10,000 and 20,000 ft. (3,000–6,000 m).*

► *Big white puffy clouds are called cumulus clouds. They may expand into stratocumulus, which form sheets of cloud, with gray patches. From above, they look white and puffy.*

▲ *Altostratus is a white or gray sheet of cloud at a height of between 10,000 and 20,000 ft. (3,000–6,000 m). It is composed mainly of water droplets, but may also contain ice crystals.*

◄ *Stratus cloud is a low-altitude, flat-looking gray sheet.*

◄ *Nimbostratus is a very low stratus cloud from which rain falls.*

▶ *The Sun heats some parts of the ground, such as rock or bare soil, more than others. On warm days, bubbles of hot air form over these areas, and they rise up through the cooler air around them.*

HOW CLOUDS FORM

The amount of water vapor air can hold depends on the temperature of the air. If warm, moist air is cooled, its water vapor will condense. This is why water condenses on a cold window. Clouds form when the water vapor condenses around tiny solid particles.

▲ *At night, fog forms as warm air is chilled by contact with a cold valley floor. As the ground warms again the fog lifts to form low cloud.*

▶ *The warm air rises into low-pressure air and expands and cools. The air cools so much that the water vapor condenses into droplets, and a small cumulus cloud is formed.*

FOG

Fog is cloud that forms close to the ground. The different types of fog are named after the ways in which they are formed. Advection fog forms when warm, moist air passes over cold ground or water. Radiation fog forms at night, as the land cools and the air above it is chilled.

▶ *The cloud grows if it is fed by a series of air bubbles, and the wind detaches it. Fair-weather cumulus looks like cotton balls. It does not carry enough water to cause rain.*

▼ *Advection fogs are common in San Francisco, rolling in from the Pacific to envelop the Golden Gate Bridge. They form when warm, moist air from the south meets cold ocean currents from the Arctic. In the daytime, the air over the warm land is at low pressure and a sea breeze carries the fog ashore.*

▼ *Moist air that rises over a mountain and then sinks again may set up waves in the air downwind of the mountain. As the air rises to the crest of a wave, it cools and clouds are formed in the shape of a lens. They are called "lenticular" clouds.*

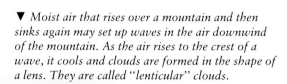

FACTS ABOUT CLOUDS

Cloud names are easy to remember:
• Those that begin with **alto-** form at medium height, between 6,500 and 20,000 ft. (2,000–6,000 m).
• Those beginning **cirr-** form above 20,000 ft. (6,000 m). Clouds without these prefixes form below 6,500 ft. (2,000 m).
• **Strat-** clouds form flat-looking layers; those with **cumu-** form heaps.

• **Nimb-** means a rain cloud.
• The highest standard cloud formation is cirrus, up to 40,000 ft. (12,000 m), but nacreous cloud may form at almost 80,000 ft. (24,000 m).
• Sea-level fogs on the Grand Banks in Newfoundland persist for 120 days of the year.
• Aircraft often produce trails of cloud at high altitudes, when water vapor from the hot engine exhaust condenses.

Rain and Snow

Water that falls from a cloud is called "precipitation" and may take the form of rain, drizzle, hail, sleet, or snow. Not all precipitation reaches the ground. In warm weather, rain may fall from a cloud only to evaporate again in midair.

Whether precipitation falls as water, ice, or a mixture of the two, depends on the conditions inside the cloud and the temperature of the air outside it. In summer, most of the ice that forms inside a cloud melts as it falls, except during the occasional hailstorm.

SNOW CRYSTALS
When water freezes, its molecules bind together into flat, six-sided crystals with four long sides and two short ones. The crystal grows as other water molecules attach themselves to its six sides. Each snowflake is unique.

RAIN AND SNOW
There are two main types of rain. In the tropics, rain is formed when air currents cause the tiny water droplets in a cloud to bump into each other. These droplets join together to form larger drops which fall as rain. Most rain outside the tropics is caused by snowflakes melting as they fall. The height at which water freezes as it condenses out of a cloud is called the "freezing level." The ice crystals grow rapidly into snowflakes as water droplets freeze onto them. If the freezing level is below 1,000 ft. (300 m), the ice crystals will not have time to melt before reaching the ground and will fall as snow.

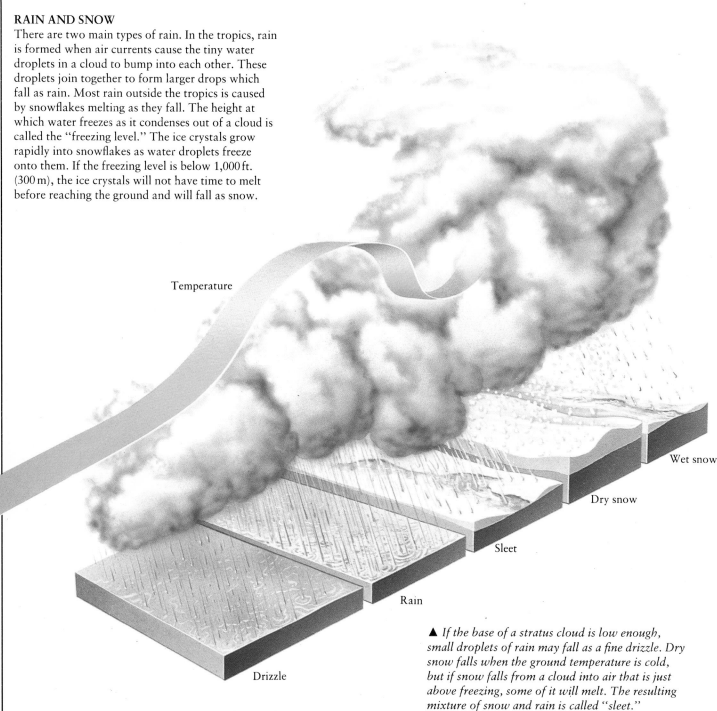

Temperature

Drizzle

Rain

Sleet

Dry snow

Wet snow

▲ *If the base of a stratus cloud is low enough, small droplets of rain may fall as a fine drizzle. Dry snow falls when the ground temperature is cold, but if snow falls from a cloud into air that is just above freezing, some of it will melt. The resulting mixture of snow and rain is called "sleet."*

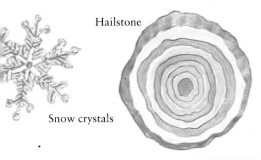

Hailstone

Snow crystals

Hailstone

HAILSTONES

Hailstones form around a small ice crystal. Alternate layers of clear and milky ice build up as the hailstones are swept up and float down inside the cloud.

▶ Some very cold clouds can be made to release rain by dropping crystals of silver iodide or dry ice into them. Water then freezes onto the crystals. This is called "seeding" the cloud, and has been used to end droughts.

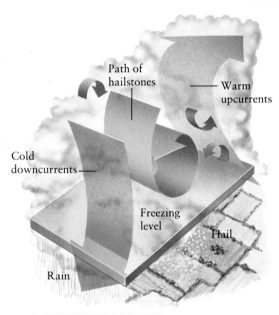

Path of hailstones

Warm upcurrents

Cold downcurrents

Freezing level

Hail

Rain

SUN'S HALO

When a thin veil of cloud partly covers the Sun, light rays may be refracted (bent) by the ice crystals. This creates a "halo," a ring of white light around the Sun, sometimes with a faint tinge of red on the inside and violet on the outside. Small water droplets in such clouds as altocumulus can also refract light, making a colored "corona," usually blue on the inside and red on the outside. A white halo can also occur when cirrus clouds obscure the Moon.

RAINBOWS AND FOGBOWS

A rainbow is caused by sunlight, or even moonlight, shining on a screen of water droplets. Rays are refracted as they enter a droplet, reflected from the back of the droplet, and then refracted a second time. Light of different wavelengths is refracted by different amounts, which splits the white light into its rainbow colors. A secondary rainbow, with the order of its colors reversed, may appear outside the primary rainbow. A fogbow is similar, but its colors overlap and mix to produce white.

HOW HAIL IS FORMED

Inside a storm cloud, raindrops may be carried up by air currents and frozen high in the cloud. An opaque layer of ice builds up as water vapor freezes onto them. They fall to warmer levels, where the outside melts and is then refrozen into a clear layer of ice as the hailstone is carried up again. The hailstone rises and falls until it is heavy enough to fall out of the cloud.

▶ In 1970, hailstones weighing 27 oz. (760 g) fell in Kansas. In 1928 a hailstone measuring 5.5 in. (14 cm) across and weighing 25 oz. (700 g) fell in Nebraska.

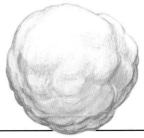

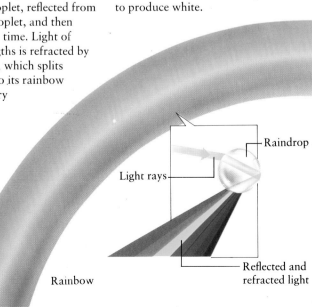

Raindrop

Light rays

Reflected and refracted light

Rainbow

Weather Forecasting

We all like to know what the weather will be like over the next few hours or days. Indeed, it is very important for some people to know. Farmers must know when to plow or harvest their crops. Fishermen must know whether it is safe for them to leave port. Aircraft pilots must know what weather they will encounter during a flight, so that they can avoid dangers such as large thunderstorms. Scientists who study the weather are called meteorologists, and much of their work involves preparing weather forecasts.

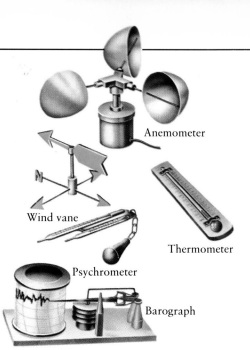

Anemometer

Wind vane

Thermometer

Psychrometer

Barograph

WEATHER SYMBOLS

Weather maps summarize conditions at a particular time. They are called "synoptic charts" and use standard symbols. The most prominent of these symbols are "isobars," the lines connecting places where air pressure is the same. Winds flow roughly parallel to the isobars. The closer together the isobars are, the stronger the wind. The chart also shows warm and cold fronts (*see page 53*).

WEATHER INSTRUMENTS

Meteorologists use a barograph, a barometer linked to a pen and paper drum, to record atmospheric pressure. A thermometer records temperature, and a wind vane and anemometer record wind direction and speed. Wet- and dry-bulb thermometers (psychrometers) measure humidity.

▲ *A weather map may show the pressure (in millibars) on isobars and at centers of low and high pressure.*

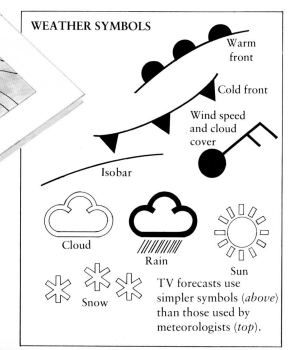

WEATHER SYMBOLS

Warm front

Cold front

Wind speed and cloud cover

Isobar

Cloud

Rain

Sun

Snow

TV forecasts use simpler symbols (*above*) than those used by meteorologists (*top*).

COLORS IN THE SKY

There is a scientific explanation for much weather lore. If the wind is from the west, a red sky at sunset means the air to the west is dry and the next day is likely to be fine. If it is dull red with cloud, there may soon be rain. A red sky in the morning means clouds are arriving and the day may be rainy.

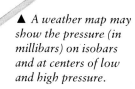

WEATHER TRACKING

Forecasters know the kind of weather associated with different cloud types. Cloud patterns often indicate areas of high and low pressure. By tracking weather systems, from surface reports and satellite images, meteorologists can predict their movements and speeds and the ways they will change. It is essential that the path of a hurricane is predicted accurately, so that people in threatened areas can be evacuated. Unfortunately, hurricane systems are so complicated that this is not always possible.

▲ *Weather planes monitor conditions in the upper atmosphere, using instruments attached to the aircraft's long nose. Conditions at sea are reported by specially equipped ocean weather ships (left). These ships are towed to positions far from shipping lanes, where they are anchored; they send reports up to eight times a day.*

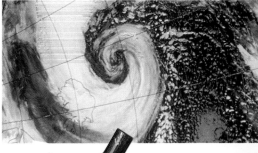

▲ *Weather satellites (left) transmit photographs of cloud patterns back to Earth, allowing scientists to study their type and movement. Satellites traveling in geostationary orbit remain above one point on the surface. Others orbit from pole to pole.*

Meteosat

Helium balloon

Secondary balloon

▼ *In temperate climates, a piece of dry seaweed will absorb moisture from damp air. It becomes wet as humidity increases, indicating the approach of a warm front and, therefore rain. It dries as the warm air passes.*

Kelp

CHAOS THEORY

Meteorologists are able to prepare a weather forecast for only a few days ahead. Long-range forecasts proved so unreliable that meteorologists no longer do them. The problem is that local differences in conditions, which are too small to record, can greatly alter the way a weather system moves and develops. So, for example, a small change in the air over the Arctic could cause a hurricane in the tropics. Scientists use a theory known as the "chaos" theory to describe this unpredictable behavior.

▶ *Balloons called "radiosondes" carry instruments that are able to measure the temperature, pressure, and humidity of the upper atmosphere. The readings are sent by radio from the balloon to ground weather stations. The flight of some balloons, called "rawinsondes," is tracked. These balloons are filled with helium, and they expand as they rise into less dense air. Their path reveals the speed and direction of winds at high altitudes.*

Instrument package

61

LANDSCAPES

The Changing Scene

The world's different landscapes have been made mainly by the action of the weather on rocks. Over thousands of years, mountains are worn away by wind, ice, and rain, until they become gently rolling hills and, eventually, level plains. As the rocks are broken into tiny fragments, living organisms can obtain the minerals they need from them, providing that they also have water. These organisms convert the mineral particles into soil. Plants grow in the soil, and animals can feed on the plants. Farmers may clear away the natural vegetation to plow fields and grow crops, where the soil and climate are suitable. Climate variations are recorded in the landscapes the farmers have formed. The hills, valleys, and soils of a desert are different from those of a forest, but plants may grow in soils that formed millions of years ago in a desert.

WORLD VEGETATION

The Earth can be divided into regions that have roughly the same climate. On land, it is mainly the climate that determines the kinds of plants that grow naturally in an area. Similar types of vegetation cover vast areas—these are called "biomes."

The tropical rain forest biome forms a belt on either side of the equator. Subtropical grasslands give way to scrub and semi-arid grassland, then to hot deserts, just outside the tropics. Beyond the tropics, temperate grasslands give way to temperate forests, then conifers, tundra, and eventually permanent ice.

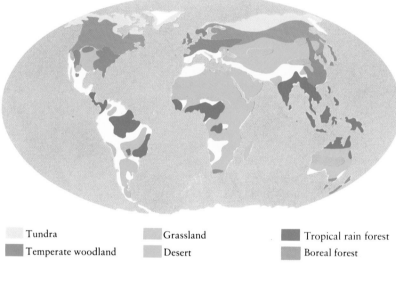

Tundra

Temperate woodland

Grassland

Desert

Tropical rain forest

Boreal forest

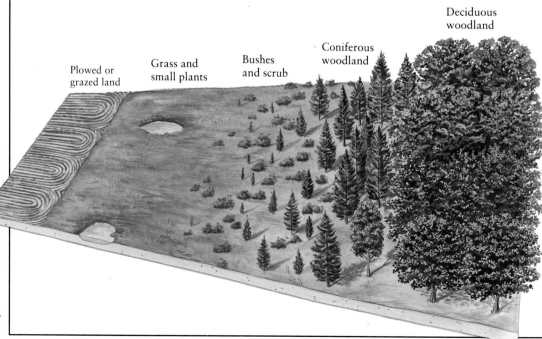

Plowed or grazed land

Grass and small plants

Bushes and scrub

Coniferous woodland

Deciduous woodland

◀ *In a temperate climate bare land will not remain so for any length of time. The first plants to colonize are small herbs that grow quickly. These herbs are soon followed by grasses, which grow tall enough to shelter the seedlings of woody plants, such as blackberry bushes, and small trees, such as hawthorn and hazel. Then larger trees appear, such as beech and oak. This sequence is called a "succession."*

LAND USE

In Europe, the first villages were built near rivers, which supplied fish and fresh water. Later, forests were cleared to make fields for crops and grazing animals. The early farms grew until most of the valleys were cultivated. By the 11th century most of the original forest had disappeared, and many riverside settlements became large towns. Rock and metal ores were mined before Roman times.

Prehistoric

Medieval

◀ *Until people settled down and began to clear the land for fields and cut trees for houses, they had little impact on the landscape.*

▶ *In the 18th to 19th centuries as industry grew, so did the towns and the demand for raw materials and coal. The countryside became dirty and ugly. Today development continues, but we are aware of the damage we can do.*

18th–19th Century

Today

SOIL

The rate at which rock is changed into soil depends mainly on the climate. In places where the ground is frozen for most of the time, soil forms very slowly. The soils in the far north of America and Asia are said to be "young," because their formation has barely begun. Near the equator, where the climate is warm and wet, soils form rapidly and are said to be "ancient."

Scientists group different soil types into 10 orders. The very young ones are called Inceptisols, the ancient ones are Oxisols or Ultisols. Desert soils, also called Aridisols, are poorly developed because of the shortage of water and the lack of decomposed remains of plants (humus), which help make a soil fertile.

The best farm soils are the Mollisols of the prairies and steppes, and the Spodosols of temperate forests, found in northeastern North America and Britain.

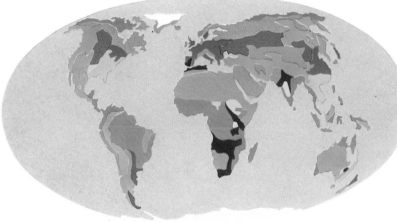

- Tundra soils
- Podzols (Spodosols)
- Podzols and Brown Earths (Spodosols and Inceptisols)
- Podzols (Spodosols)
- Chernozems (Mollisols)
- Alfisols
- Grumusols (Vertisols)
- Desert soils (Aridisols)
- Ferralsols (Oxisols)
- Montane soils

Zonal soil types (shown above) were based on climatic factors. New names given in parentheses.

SOIL PROFILES

Once a soil has developed it forms layers, called "horizons." Beneath a surface layer of plant remains, the A horizon is rich in decomposed organic plant and animal matter. The B horizon is mainly mineral particles, with much less organic material. The C horizon is primarily small stones, and beneath them all lies the bedrock.

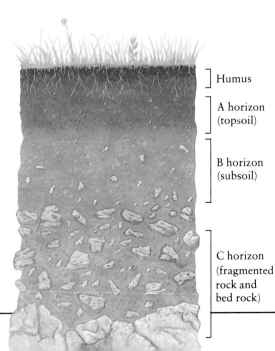

Humus

A horizon (topsoil)

B horizon (subsoil)

C horizon (fragmented rock and bed rock)

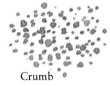

Blocky

Prismatic

Platy

Crumb

▲ *The amount of air and water found in a soil depends on the particles from which it is made. A platy structure packs into watertight layers. A blocky structure drains well, a prismatic one less well. A crumb structure is best of all.*

Polar Regions and the Tundra

Within the Arctic and Antarctic circles there is at least one day a year when the Sun does not rise, and at least one when it does not set. The Arctic and Antarctic are lands of midnight Sun in summer, and noon darkness in winter. The polar regions are the coldest on Earth, and among the driest because there is little liquid water. Most of Greenland lies beneath ice 5,000 ft. (1,500 m) thick, that fills valleys and buries hills. The average thickness of the Antarctic ice sheet is more than 6,500 ft. (2,000 m).

ICEBERGS

An iceberg is a large block of floating ice. It is much larger than it looks because some nine-tenths of the ice floats below the surface. This can be dangerous to ships. Some Antarctic icebergs are more than 60 mi. (100 km) long.

THE ARCTIC AND THE ANTARCTIC

Most of Greenland and the northern parts of Alaska, Canada, Scandinavia, and Siberia lie within the Arctic Circle, but there is no land close to the North Pole itself. Antarctica is the world's fifth largest continent, divided into two parts by the Transantarctic Mountains. Beneath the ice, the land of East Antarctica is mostly rugged, in places rising to more than 13,000 ft. (4,000 m) above sea level. West Antarctica is lower. Much of it is made up of a peninsula and island archipelago. In places, the land around the South Pole is up to 8,200 ft. (2,500 m) below sea level.

THE TUNDRA

Around the Arctic Circle, between the conifer forests farther south and the region of permanent ice to the north, the tundra extends as a vast treeless plain across all the northern continents. In summer the ground thaws for just a few weeks, triggering frantic activity for the region's animals and plants.

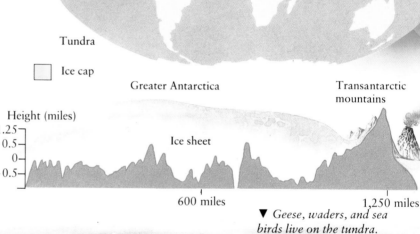

Tundra

☐ Ice cap

Greater Antarctica

Transantarctic mountains

Height (miles)

1.25
0.5
0
−0.5

Ice sheet

600 miles   1,250 miles

▼ *Geese, waders, and sea birds live on the tundra. Tundra mammals include polar and grizzly bears, musk ox, caribou, voles, and shrews.*

Pingo

Dwarf birch

Lichen

◄ *Tundra plants are small, as their roots can only grow to a depth of 12 in. (30 cm) before they reach frozen ground. There are heaths, dwarf birch trees, sedges and rushes, mosses and lichens. Many plants flower in the brief summer.*

Sea level

FACTS ABOUT POLAR LANDS

- During the dark nights, plant nutrients accumulate in the sea. As the light returns, marine plants multiply rapidly, providing food for small and larger animals, such as fish, sea birds, seals, and whales.
- Each year, more than 7,000 icebergs are carried south from Greenland in the Labrador Current.

Glacier or ice sheet

| Pack ice |
| Drift ice |
| Ice shelves |
| Ice sheet |
| – – – Tree line |

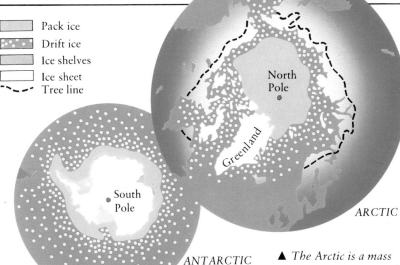

North Pole

Greenland

ARCTIC

South Pole

ANTARCTIC

▲ *Where a glacier enters the sea, the ice floats on the water. The end of the glacier snaps off to form an iceberg. Ice shelfs also break, forming much larger icebergs.*

▼ *Under the Antarctic ice sheet, unlike the Arctic, there is land. Near the coasts some glaciers have retreated, leaving dry, rocky valleys, called "oases." Inland, high mountain peaks project above the ice, as "nunataks."*

▲ *The extent of the Antarctic ice sheet varies with the changing seasons. In winter the drift ice extends out to the southern tip of South America. The Antarctic is home to a few plants and some insects. In summer, penguins, sea birds, and seals visit it.*

▲ *The Arctic is a mass of pack ice which also changes with the seasons. In winter, its ice covers all of Greenland and its drift ice reaches as far south as Iceland and northern Russia. The presence of the ice and tundra lands limits the growth of trees to areas south of the line through northern Canada, Norway, Sweden, and Russia.*

Lesser Antarctica

Ross Ice Shelf

Ice sheet

2,000 miles   2,500 miles   3,000 miles

Soil thaws in summer

Permafrost

PERMAFROST

In winter, in the Arctic and Antarctic, all the moisture in the soil freezes, but in some areas the top few inches of the soil thaw in summer. During the summer thaw, the ground turns to mud, with pools in the hollows. The subsoil and deeper layers remain permanently frozen. They are called "permafrost." If the permafrost thaws, for example, because of the heating effect of a house or oil pipeline, then the land will sink.

POLAR RESOURCES

Long ago, the polar regions lay in lower latitudes and had warmer climates. In Antarctica, there are deposits of coal up to 20 ft. (6 m) thick, formed 250 million years ago. Alaska also has vast coal reserves, and, in 1968, one of the world's largest oil fields was discovered at Prudhoe Bay.

▼ *Oil travels south from Alaska to ports by the Trans-Alaska Pipeline. The pipeline was built on supports above the ground, to prevent it thawing the permafrost.*

Temperate Woodland

During the last Ice Age, most of the northern latitudes, higher than 50°, lay beneath ice. When the ice retreated, it left bare rock and debris. As the climate warmed up, groups of plants spread north, until most of the landscape was covered by forest. Trees in far northern regions have to survive the equivalent of a dry season, when water is frozen. Deciduous trees save water by shedding leaves, conifers have needle-like leaves from which little water evaporates. Both types form large areas of forest.

SOIL
Soils of conifer forests have a light-colored, rather acid upper layer. Some soil minerals dissolve and drain into the subsoil. Broadleaved forests develop very fertile soil with an even, brown surface layer.

WOODLAND AREAS
Broadleaved evergreen forests grow around the Mediterranean and in those regions of the southern United States, China, South America, South Africa, and southern Australia, where temperatures rarely fall below freezing. Broadleaved deciduous forests grow farther north. Southern Chile is the only place they are found in the Southern Hemisphere. Most of Canada, northern Europe, and Asia is covered by coniferous or boreal forest. There is no boreal forest in the Southern Hemisphere.

Temperate woodland

THE FOREST ECOSYSTEM
The trees of the broadleaved evergreen forest include holm oak, cork oak, and a few species, such as holly, that also grow in mild, moist regions farther north. These species are usually mixed with pines and cedars. The deciduous forests have a wider variety of species. They are often dominated by oak, beech, and maple, with different species in Europe and North America. Coniferous forest is made up entirely of pines, spruces, firs, and larches. Each type of forest has its own type of wildlife. The evergreen forests have fewer animal species than the others. Species found in the conifer forests include moose, bears, and wolves.

◄ Near the edges of the temperate deciduous forest area, conifers grow side by side with broadleaved trees. This mixed forest of aspens and larch is in the Nevada Rockies. North American woodlands contain more tree species than European woodlands. The richest deciduous forests are in the Appalachians, in the east. The species include tulip trees and oaks, and basswood and buckeye.

Mixed woodland

WOODLANDS

- Approximately 29 percent of the United States is forested, compared to 24 percent of Western Europe. About 850 native and naturalized species of trees are grown in the U.S.
- All the paper we use comes from conifers grown in temperate regions.

DEFORESTATION IN EUROPE

Most of the original forest that once covered Europe was cleared long ago to provide farmland. In Britain, this clearance was well advanced by the end of the Roman occupation. By the 11th century, trees covered a smaller area than they do today. The woodlands that remained were made up of species that had established themselves naturally. Some of these survive as "ancient woodlands." These are woods where trees have grown since before the forest plantations were begun in the 18th century. Scientists identify them from historical records, and also by the type of plant species they contain.

Natural extent of forest

Present extent of forest

▲ *The New England forests are famous for their autumn colors. As leaves die, they lose their green chlorophyll, revealing many shades of red and yellow.*

Deciduous woodland

▲ *A European broadleaved forest typically contains oak, ash, beech, and chestnut. The trees provide shelter and food for many species of birds, insects, and small mammals. For example, the common European oak (*Quercus robur*) is said to support more than 300 animal species.*

THE NITROGEN CYCLE

Nitrogen is constantly being recycled. All proteins contain atoms of nitrogen. The nitrogen is taken from the air by soil bacteria and made into soluble nitrate ("fixed"), which is absorbed by plants. Other bacteria decompose organic matter, releasing nitrate and returning some nitrogen to the air.

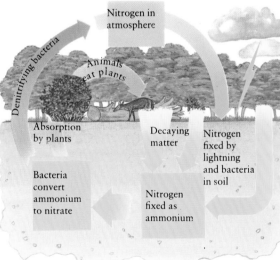

Nitrogen in atmosphere

Denitrifying bacteria

Animals eat plants

Absorption by plants

Decaying matter

Nitrogen fixed by lightning and bacteria in soil

Bacteria convert ammonium to nitrate

Nitrogen fixed as ammonium

▲ *Nitrogen passes from air to soil, to plants, to animals which eat plants, and eventually back into the air. The energy of lightning also fixes some nitrogen, by making the gas react with oxygen to form nitrogen oxides. These dissolve in rain. Some nitrate drains from the soil into rivers and then into the sea. This supplies nitrogen for freshwater and marine plants, and the animals that feed on them.*

Grasslands

There are regions where, for most of the year, the rate at which water can evaporate is greater than the amount of rainfall. Such regions would be deserts, were it not for the rain that falls during one season of the year. Just beyond the edges of the deserts, rain falls in the summer. In the dry interior of continents it falls in winter. The rain allows plants to grow, turning the dry, brown landscape green. Few trees can survive in these conditions, but flowering herbs and grasses abound. These regions are the grasslands.

SOIL
Grassland soils have a deep, dark-colored, surface layer rich in humus. They are among the most fertile of all soils and are often farmed. The lower layers vary from place to place.

GRASSLANDS OF THE WORLD
The middle of continents are dry, because of their distance from the sea. The temperate, continental grasslands are called "steppes" in Europe and Asia, "prairies" in North America, and "pampas" in South America. Temperate grassland is also found in eastern Australia. The subtropical grasslands of South America, Africa, India, and northern Australia are called "savanna."

Grassland vegetation is mainly made up of drought-resistant grasses. In parts of the steppe these grasses are short, but they can be up to 7 ft. (2 m) tall. Grass leaves grow from the base and can survive and grow even if grazed.

Grasslands

THE LANDSCAPES
In the rainy season, grasses and herbs grow rapidly. The land turns green or is blanketed by a mass of brightly colored flowers. The flowers set seed quickly and then die, with nutrients stored in their roots. As the rains stop, the plants turn brown. The dry vegetation burns easily and fires are common.

The fires nourish the soil with ash, which encourages new growth next time it rains. The plants have deep roots.

In Europe, the climate and geography have led to forests as the natural landscape, and almost all grassland has been reclaimed from forest.

▼ *Much of the South American pampas is covered by tussocks, or humps of feather grass. Elsewhere there is scrub. Underneath the plants the ground is hard.*

Prairie

Pampas

Prairie grass

◄ *The prairies were once home to large herds of bison (buffalo). Today, most of the prairie is used to grow wheat and corn.*

◄ *Grasslands differ mainly by the species in each location. In Australia, the grasslands cover a wide range of soils and feature tough grasses and scattered acacia and gum trees. These grasslands are home to kangaroos, koalas, emus, and kookaburras.*

SLASH AND BURN

People have extended grasslands by setting fire to vegetation during the dry season. This encourages new growth, but destroys woody plants. Livestock also destroy tree seedlings by trampling them.

Kopje

Bornhardt

THE DUST BOWL

The grassland climate is dry and sometimes there are long droughts. One in the prairies of the central United States lasted from 1933 to 1939. Severe dust storms in 1934 and 1935 turned the area into what came to be known as the "Dust Bowl." The situation had been made worse by years of overgrazing and poor farming.

▲ *On the African savanna, domed rock formations called "bornhardts" stand above the plateau. These are made of granite or similar rock. The round shape results from curved sheets of rock that are separating from the solid rock underneath. There are other small, isolated hills about 30 ft. (10 m) tall formed from exposed rock. They are called castle "kopjes" (pronounced koppies).*

Savanna

Umbrella tree

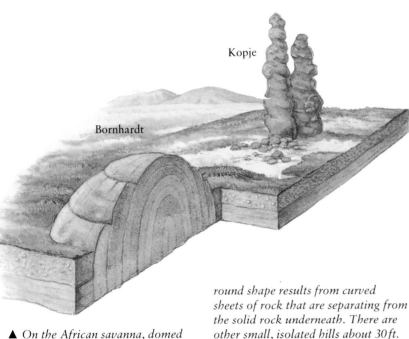

Red oat grass

▲ *African savanna is found on both sides of the equator. It is home to many species of grazing animals, such as wildebeest which move in large herds. Each species feeds differently, so they do not compete with each other. The grazers provide food for lions, cheetahs, hyenas, dogs, and other carnivores. Not all African grasslands are tropical savanna, the South African "veld" is temperate grassland.*

FACTS ABOUT GRASSLANDS

- Grasslands are cultivated in North America and to a limited extent in Europe, but farming is restricted by the dry climate.
- In South America and Australia the grasslands are used for cattle ranching.
- The southern part of the African savanna is farmed, but over most of the area people live mainly by herding cattle. In the dry season people and cattle move around in search of pasture, as do all grazing animals.
- Wheat is grown on the Indian savanna.
- There are nearly 8,000 species of grasses. Some have roots that can reach water 16 ft. (5 m) below ground.

Deserts

When rain falls on the ground some of it evaporates. If the amount of water that evaporates is greater than the rainfall, a desert will form. Any region where the annual rainfall is less than 10 in. (250 mm) is a desert. Deserts are usually windy, but not necessarily hot. The polar regions are deserts, and temperatures in the Gobi Desert are below freezing for 6 months of every year. Most deserts are rocky not sandy. Sand covers about 2 percent of the North American desert, and only 11 percent of the Sahara.

► *Many plants survive in the desert by having a very fast life cycle. Their seeds can lie dormant for many years. On the rare occasions of rainfall, these plants, such as this African grass, germinate, flower, set seed, and die, all in a matter of days.*

Before rain

After rain

ARID LANDS

Deserts are also known as arid or dry lands. Desert soils contain almost no plant or animal (organic) matter. They are made up of dry sand grains and stones, often with gravel, because wind blows away smaller particles. Some desert soils can be cultivated, if water is provided. Most of the world's hot deserts are spreading, mostly due to a change in climate, bringing drier weather to bordering lands. Overgrazing may make this worse by removing vegetation, causing soil erosion.

Arid areas

DESERT ECOSYSTEMS

Few plants can grow in shifting sand. There are two main types of desert plants. Shrubs and small trees—such as the Joshua trees, saguaro cactus trees, and sagebrushes of North America and the acacias and tamarisks of the Sahara—store water. Others lie dormant waiting for rain.

► *The constant sand-laden wind sculpts rocks into strange shapes. The rocks are also heated by the Sun— they expand, and then cool and shrink. This strain splits them.*

Joshua tree

Saguaro

Prickly pear

Dry river bed

Stony desert

Rock pavement

SAND DUNES

Many different types of sand dunes are formed in sandy deserts. They are shaped by the wind. A "barchan" has a crescent-shaped front and a long tail made from sand blown by the wind. They form long series. "Linear" dunes are created in strong steady winds, which cut troughs in the desert floor. The sand is piled up into long, rounded dunes. A "seif" dune is a long, sharp ridge lying parallel to the wind direction. A ridge that is formed at right angles to the wind is an "aklé" dune. It is formed where there are cross currents. "Star" dunes, with several sharp ridges, occur where the wind direction is constantly changing.

Barchan

Linear dune

FACTS ABOUT DESERTS

● In some hot deserts, a "sand sea" may form, called an "erg." The biggest is the Grand Erg Oriental, covering 76,000 sq. mi. (196,000 sq. km) in Algeria and Tunisia. Some dunes in the Grand Erg are more than 1,000 ft. (300 m) high.

● Death Valley, in the Mojave Desert of California, is the hottest place in North America. Summer temperatures often exceed 120°F (50°C), and 135°F (57°C) has been recorded. Temperatures are similar in the Libyan Sahara, where 136°F (58°C) has been recorded. Desert nights are cool.

● The coldest place in the world is in Antarctica, which is also a desert. The winter temperature can fall to −130°F (−90°C).

▼ *High, rocky Saharan plateaus (hamada) are cut through by deep canyons.*

Hamada

Mesa

Sand dunes

Salt pan

Sandy desert

Oasis

▼ *Oases are natural desert features, but people can make them. In places where water lies close to the surface wells are dug, and the underground water from distant wetter regions is released under pressure from the aquifer.*

OASES

An oasis is a fertile place in a desert where the water table reaches the surface. Sometimes water will fill an aquifer (a rock that holds water). If there is a fault above the aquifer the water will be forced up it and an oasis will form.

◄ *A stony desert, or the surface of small, rounded pebbles, is called a "reg."*

Oasis

Saturated sand

Fault

Impermeable rock

Aquifer

Impermeable rock

Tropical Rain Forests

The ice sheets have advanced and retreated many times over land near the poles. But in a belt of land around the equator the temperature has never fallen below freezing. As the climate changed near the poles, so did the forests. But in the tropics, forest of one kind or another has grown in some places for millions of years. In this time, species have evolved to fill every corner and use every source of food. This is why tropical rain forests contain a greater variety of plant and animal species than any other forests.

SOILS

Tropical soils are red or yellow in color and up to 33 ft. (10 m) deep. They lie on top of clay. Most nutrients have been lost from the surface layers. Plants feed on the rapidly recycled organic matter.

HUMID HABITATS

The equatorial climate is warm, with heavy rainfall. Plants grow rapidly, and in order to expose their leaves to sunlight, trees grow very tall. The tops of the trees form a continuous canopy, at a height of about 130 ft. (40 m), shading the ground. Most of the trees have shallow roots. They obtain their nutrients from the uppermost layer of soil. Many support themselves with roots that grow outward as stilts or props. Smaller trees and seedlings form a lower layer of forest, and shrubs grow near ground level.

■ Tropical rain forest

THE ECOSYSTEM

Rain forest grows in lowland areas, including shallow swamps. But much of the equatorial region is mountainous. As you go higher, the lowland forest changes into forest with smaller trees. There is more abundant undergrowth, often with palms, and many more plants growing at ground level. This is called "montane" forest. Higher still, the forest becomes more open. The trees are shorter and covered in epiphytes and climbers. Mosses, ferns, and herbs blanket the ground. This is called "cloud" forest because it is often shrouded in low cloud, from which it obtains moisture.

FACTS ABOUT RAIN FORESTS

● When tropical forest is cleared, new growth often forms a dense "jungle."

● Because of the shade in a rain forest, the air temperature may not be high. But the lack of wind and high humidity make it feel hotter.

● Despite the high rainfall, in most places the ground dries out quickly.

● Tropical forests are being cleared mainly to provide land for farming and plantation forestry. This is often successful on richer soils in valleys, but elsewhere crops soon fail as surface nutrients are removed.

EROSION

When trees are cleared from a hillside the soil may be left bare. Rain can then wash away topsoil, which is carried down the slope. Sometimes it falls into a river, causing pollution.

◄ *In Colombia, as elsewhere in the tropics, isolated hills with steep, smooth sides rise 1,300 ft. (400 m) or more above the plains. These "inselbergs," or "sugar-loaf mountains," are made from layers of rock that have separated and are peeling away.*

▲ *In Madagascar, most of the original rain forest has been cut down to provide land for growing crops. Removing the protective forest cover has caused severe soil erosion.*

Inselberg

◄ *The crowns, or tops, of trees in the rain forest merge to form an interlocking canopy of leafy vegetation about 145 ft. (44 m) from the ground. Food is more abundant here than on the ground, and many of the snakes, lizards, frogs, birds, mammals, and insects living here never visit the ground.*

MANGROVE SWAMPS

Mangrove forests form dense thickets in coastal swamps. The trees produce stilt roots which then develop more roots of their own. Some of these roots stick out above the mud in which they grow. The roots trap shifting sediment, gradually extending the land seaward. Snails and other small animals live among the roots.

PAST, PRESENT, FUTURE

Natural Resources: Energy

Substances we use to make the things we need are called "resources." To prepare a meal, for example, we need food, water, pots and pans, cutlery, an oven, and a source of heat. The food and water, the metals from which the oven and utensils are made, and the fuel that is burned to produce heat are all resources. They are called natural resources because we obtain them from the world around us. If using a resource does not reduce the amount of it available to us, it is called a "renewable" resource. River water is a renewable resource, provided we take no more of it than is replaced by the rain. Food is a renewable resource because farmers can grow more. Most of our energy resources are "nonrenewable," either because the amount of the resource is fixed and cannot be replaced, or because it is replaced, but only very slowly.

FOSSIL FUELS

The word "fossil" is from a Latin word meaning "dug from the ground." Coal, oil, and natural gas are called fossil fuels because they are made from the remains of ancient plants or animals. They were formed very slowly over millions of years and are nonrenewable.

▶ *Coal formed from trees and other plants that grew beside water. When the trees died, they could not rot away fully because the ground was waterlogged. They accumulated as peat and were eventually buried. The peat was squashed by its own weight and the weight of the rocks above it, making it harder, and turning into "lignite," or "brown coal."*

Movements of the rocks underneath then squashed some of the coal even more and heated it, forming a hard black coal called anthracite. Anthracite burns better than lignite as it contains more carbon.

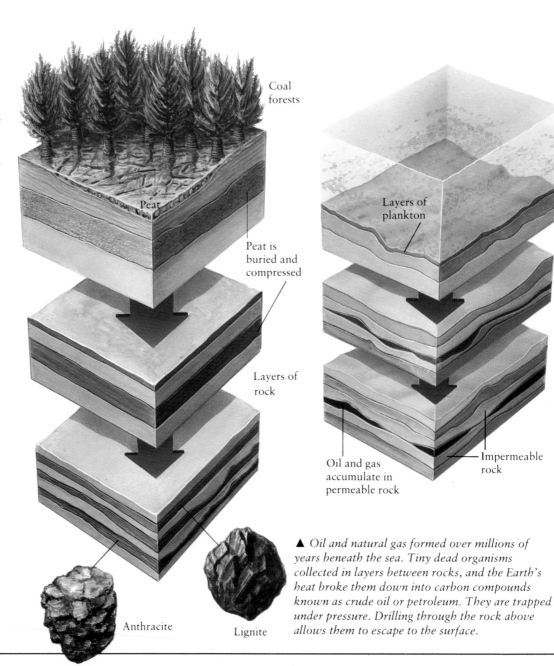

Coal forests

Peat

Peat is buried and compressed

Layers of rock

Layers of plankton

Oil and gas accumulate in permeable rock

Impermeable rock

Anthracite

Lignite

▲ *Oil and natural gas formed over millions of years beneath the sea. Tiny dead organisms collected in layers between rocks, and the Earth's heat broke them down into carbon compounds known as crude oil or petroleum. They are trapped under pressure. Drilling through the rock above allows them to escape to the surface.*

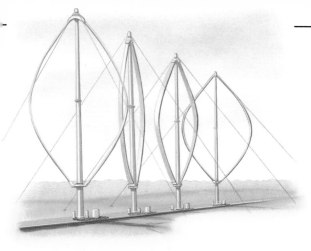

WIND POWER

Wind generators convert the motion of wind into electrical power. Wind is a renewable energy source, but it takes hundreds of very large, costly machines to obtain useful amounts.

GEOTHERMAL POWER

If a mass of rock or water below ground is hotter than its surroundings, the heat can be recovered as "geothermal energy." Drilling into the rock allows the hot water to flow to the surface. If the rock is dry, water is pumped down one hole, heated, and recovered from another. This resource is nonrenewable, because the rock is cooled, or the hot water is removed.

▲ *In some places, the pressure of water heated below ground forces it to the surface as a geyser (see page 21). The geyser can be capped and the steam is used to drive a turbine to produce electrical power.*

HYDROELECTRIC POWER

Hydroelectric power is generated by turbines driven by falling water. A dam is built across a river to form a lake. Gates in the dam wall allow the water to fall to the level of the river below, flowing past turbines inside the wall as it does so.

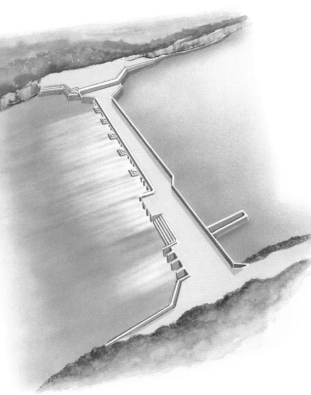

◄ *On the La Rance estuary, France, and in Fundy Bay, Canada, the ebb and flow of the tides turns turbines in a tidal barrier.*

NUCLEAR POWER

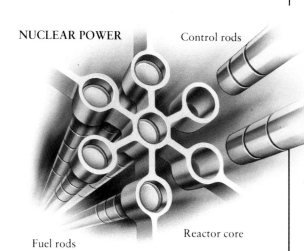

Control rods

Fuel rods

Reactor core

In the core of a nuclear reactor, uranium atoms are split to produce heat. The heat is used to boil water for steam to drive turbines. Uranium is mined from rocks.

HOW LONG WILL IT LAST?

No one knows how much of the nonrenewable resources remain. Uranium and coal will last several centuries, but oil and gas are less abundant and may soon run out.

 Oil 45 years

 Gas 76 years

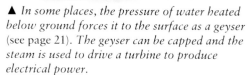

Coal 521 years

SOLAR POWER

Solar panels absorb heat from the Sun, which warms water flowing through pipes beneath the surface of the panels. The pipes pass inside the building to the hot water tank, and heat up the water. Solar cells convert sunlight into electricity. They work in warm or cold weather.

Natural Resources: Metals, Land, and Water

Metals are extremely valuable resources. Many of the everyday articles in our homes are made from metal. A few metals, such as gold and copper, occur in the Earth's crust in pure form, as "native elements." But most are found as minerals called ores, which are chemical compounds containing a high proportion of the metal. Some of our mineral resources are nonmetals. Paper is made whiter by adding kaolin, a clay mineral. Land and water are also valuable resources.

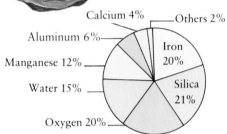

◀ *Round lumps of metal form on the bed of most oceans. In some places there are nearly 52,000 tons in a square mile. They are called "manganese nodules," but also contain other metals.*

UNDERWATER RICHES

Mineral resources are nonrenewable, although many can be recycled and used again. We obtain many minerals from quarries and mines, but the seabed and seawater itself are rich in minerals.

Manganese nodules grow very slowly on deep seabeds. They contain enough of some metals to supply us for centuries. The nodules are dredged from the seabed, but it is more costly than mining the metals on land. Phosphorus also forms nodules, which are mined off the coast of California.

Pie chart: Calcium 4%, Aluminum 6%, Manganese 12%, Water 15%, Oxygen 20%, Others 2%, Iron 20%, Silica 21%

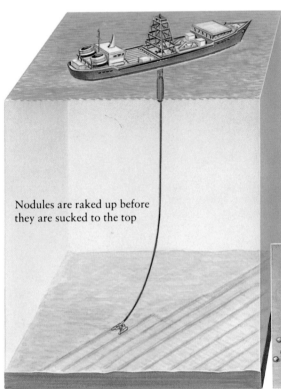

Nodules are raked up before they are sucked to the top

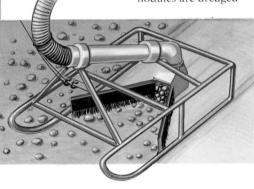

METALS

We use metals in widely differing amounts. Some, such as aluminum, iron, and magnesium, are abundant, but tin, silver, and platinum are already scarce. New deposits may be discovered, or new technology might allow existing resources to be mined more efficiently, but the costs will rise, and substitutes for some metals will be needed. The graph shows how long the known stocks of some metals may last, given the present rate of consumption.

Gold 28 years
Zinc 35 years
Nickel 75 years
Lead 40 years
Copper 60 years
Manganese 180 years
Iron ore 400 years
Bauxite (aluminum ore) 255 years

Years' supply
0   100   200   300

DATAFILE

Amount of metal produced each year worldwide (tons):
- **Iron:** 815 million
- **Bauxite (aluminum ore):** 85 million
- **Manganese:** 24 million
- **Zinc:** 7 million
- **Lead:** 3 million
- **Nickel:** 760,000
- **Copper:** 8,800
- **Gold:** 1,650
- About 15 percent by weight of the uppermost 10 mi. (16 km) of the Earth's crust is aluminum oxide.
- Sixty percent of the world's gold is mined in South Africa. The mines are up to 12,000 ft. (3,700 m) deep.

MINING ORES

Metal ores are cut or blasted from the surrounding rock. The ore is crushed, and the worthless rock removed. Many metal ores contain oxygen or sulfur. The pure metal can be separated by heating.

RARE METALS

Gold is usually found as small grains or nuggets of the pure metal. Where there is gold there may also be platinum, either pure or mixed with ores of copper, nickel, lead, or other metals. Silver occurs as a pure metal, or as silver sulfide, with the sulfides of other metals.

DRINKING WATER

In regions where rainfall is low, drinking water can be obtained by purifying seawater. The process is called "desalination," and there are two methods. The most common is distillation. Seawater is boiled and the vapor, which contains very little salt, is condensed and collected. The process is repeated until the water is fit to drink.

The other method is to force water through a membrane that allows water molecules to pass through, but traps the salts.

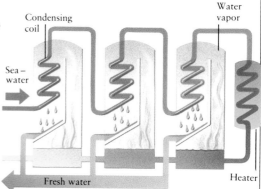

▲ *Some metals can be obtained from sands. Titanium is extracted from the rich sands on the Australian coasts.*

► *Land in the Netherlands has been reclaimed from the sea for nearly 1,000 years. About a quarter of the present land area has been created in this way.*

RECLAIMING LAND FROM THE SEA

Since medieval times, earth banks or dikes were built to protect the reclaimed Dutch "polders" from flooding. In the 1920s, a large part of the Zuider Zee in the Netherlands was reclaimed by enclosing it with a dam 18 mi. (29 km) long. The fertile polders are valuable farmland. Parts of England, Italy, and Japan have also been reclaimed.

Dams
Land reclaimed :
before 1900   after 1900

▲ *The windmills, for which the Netherlands is famous, were used to pump water from the polders into drainage channels. Continous pumping is needed as the water seeps back in.*

Air Pollution

Technology makes our lives easier, but factories, cars, and power stations also pollute the air we breathe. Incinerating waste and burning fuel to produce power releases millions of tons of gases such as carbon dioxide, sulfur dioxide, and nitrogen oxides into the air every year, together with ash, dust, and soot particles. Air pollution damages human health and harms wildlife; it can also alter the finely balanced atmospheric processes of the Earth, with potentially serious consequences.

BURNING

Although some air pollution is caused by natural sources, such as volcanic eruptions which release sulfur dioxide, most is caused by waste gases released by burning fuels and incinerating waste from homes and factories. Some of the waste contains toxic (poisonous) chemicals such as mercury which are then released into the air. Tiny particles of solids and liquids are also given off, which can cause breathing problems.

THE OZONE LAYER

Ozone is a form of oxygen in which the molecule is made up of three atoms (O_3), rather than the usual two (O_2). It forms in the stratosphere. Ultraviolet (UV) radiation from the Sun splits oxygen molecules into free oxygen atoms. Each oxygen atom joins an oxygen molecule to form ozone. UV radiation also splits ozone molecules. So ozone is constantly forming, splitting, and reforming. The UV radiation absorbed by this process cannot reach Earth. UV radiation causes sunburn, skin cancer, and eye problems; it also affects plant growth.

THE HOLE OVER THE ANTARCTIC

1979

1987

1991

◄ *Chlorine (Cl) reacts with ozone to form chlorine monoxide (ClO) and oxygen (O_2). The chlorine is then released to go around the cycle again.*

Ozone molecule (O_3)

Free chlorine atom (Cl)

Chlorine monoxide (ClO)

Oxygen molecule (O_2)

Free oxygen atom (O)

► *Every spring (October) the ozone layer over Antarctica thins by up to 50 percent. This "hole" disappears in summer, but reappears every year. In 1987 it covered an area the size of the United States. No "hole" has been detected over the Arctic, but the ozone decreases slightly in January and February.*

CFCs

Ozone is destroyed by compounds such as chlorofluorocarbons (CFCs). CFCs are used in some refrigerators and packaging materials. They drift up into the stratosphere, where they break down and release chlorine. Each chlorine atom can destroy hundreds of thousands of ozone molecules. Many scientists are concerned that as the ozone layer is damaged, a greater amount of harmful UV radiation will reach the Earth's surface.

▲ *Photochemical smog is a health hazard in many major cities. It is the result of chemical reactions caused by the action of sunlight on nitrogen oxides and unburned fuel from car exhaust fumes.*

SMOG

Earlier this century, in London and other European cities, a mixture of fog and smoke caused choking smogs, known as "pea-soupers." Today, in places where there is a lot of sunshine, such as Los Angeles, traffic fumes cause "photochemical smog."

ACID RAIN

Cloud droplets are naturally acidic, because the carbon dioxide in air dissolves to form a weak acid. But sulfur dioxide and nitrogen oxides produced by burning fossil fuels form stronger acids. The moisture reaches the ground as acid mist, snow, or rain. Acid rain damages forests and acidifies lakes, harming aquatic animals.

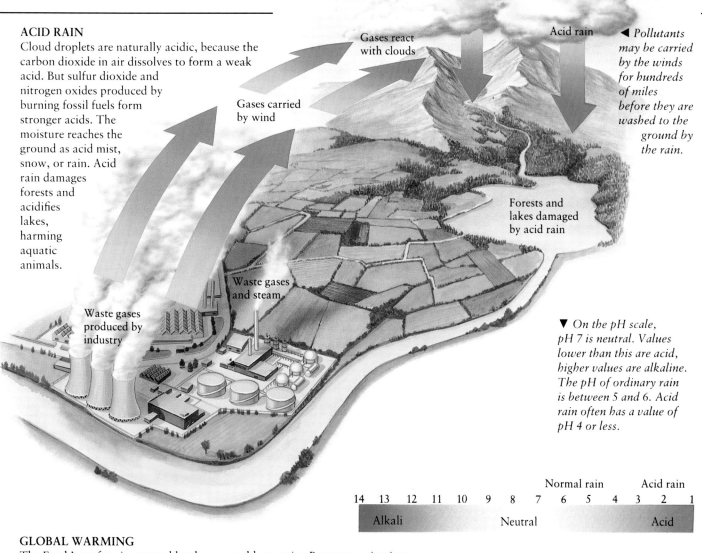

Gases react with clouds

Acid rain

Gases carried by wind

◄ *Pollutants may be carried by the winds for hundreds of miles before they are washed to the ground by the rain.*

Forests and lakes damaged by acid rain

Waste gases and steam

Waste gases produced by industry

▼ *On the pH scale, pH 7 is neutral. Values lower than this are acid, higher values are alkaline. The pH of ordinary rain is between 5 and 6. Acid rain often has a value of pH 4 or less.*

						Normal rain				Acid rain	
14	13	12	11	10	9	8	7	6	5	4	3	2	1

Alkali   Neutral   Acid

GLOBAL WARMING

The Earth's surface is warmed by the Sun and radiates heat back into space. Gases such as carbon dioxide, nitrogen oxides, methane, and CFCs in the atmosphere trap some of this heat and warm the lower atmosphere. The atmosphere radiates heat back to Earth. This is called the "greenhouse effect," and without it the Earth would be so cold that life could not exist. But many scientists fear that the huge amounts of these "greenhouse gases" released into the atmosphere by industrial processes and burning fossil fuels are warming the Earth so much that they will eventually upset the world's climate, and cause sea levels to rise.

New York

Charleston

► *Some scientists predict that the Earth's temperature could rise 5°F (3°C) by 2070. After this, the rise will level off and the temperature will stabilize. If the Antarctic ice sheet melted, sea levels could rise, threatening low-lying areas such as the U.S. coast (left).*

62.5°F

62°F

61°F

60°F

59°F

58°F

57°F

1980   2025   2070

Environmental Problems

Every living organism changes the world around it, including humans. We clear massive areas of land to grow food and to build homes, cities, and roads. We quarry and mine for building materials, minerals, and fuels, and use these to manufacture the things that improve our lives. When we are careless we harm the environment in many ways: poor people are forced to farm using methods that damage the land; we dirty water with our waste; and we harm wildlife by destroying its food and shelter.

LAND AT RISK

Land bordering all deserts is at risk. As the deserts expand, people are forced onto smaller grazing areas, increasing the risk of soil erosion. The problem is most severe in the Sahel, south of the Sahara Desert.

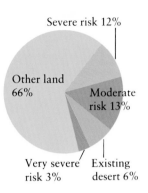

Severe risk 12%
Other land 66%
Moderate risk 13%
Very severe risk 3%
Existing desert 6%

MARCHING SAND

Much of the world's grazing land is in semi-arid areas. From time to time there are severe droughts lasting several years. During these droughts the ground dries, plants disappear, and wind-blown sand and dust may bury more fertile soil and destroy crops. Many people in the semiarid areas are nomadic, moving with the seasons in search of pasture for their animals. When the pasture fails, they are crowded into the small areas that remain. This leads to overgrazing, which causes soil erosion.

Wind

Wind direction

Lack of vegetation creates drier conditions

Irrigation

Grazing

▲ *Irrigated land grows crops, but the equipment is expensive. Unless surplus water is drained away, the ground may become waterlogged, and salts accumulate, so that crops cannot grow.*

DEFORESTATION

In the tropics, forests are cleared to provide timber. Some of the land is replanted as plantation forest and some is converted into farms and cattle ranches. Forest valleys are also flooded to make lakes for hydroelectric schemes. Plant and animal species die out; those found nowhere else become extinct.

▼ *Soil is washed into rivers, causing them to silt up.*

◄ *Clearing plants from high ground may cause flooding on low ground, as rain water quickly runs off the surface. In the dry season, exposed, infertile soils may be baked hard and crack.*

▶ *The soil in many parts of the rain forests is poor. The land can only support a few harvests before farmers have to move to a new area.*

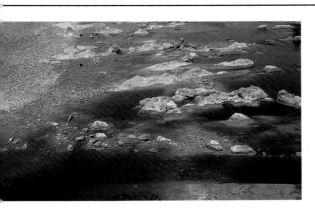

RIVERS IN PERIL
Small quantities of waste do not usually cause serious harm if they are dumped into a river, because the river quickly purifies itself. But if many factories dump their waste into the same river, it cannot cope, and the water becomes very polluted.

Oil pipeline
5 days
9 days
50 days

Spread of oil slick

EXXON VALDEZ
On March 24, 1989, the tanker *Exxon Valdez* ran aground in Alaska, releasing about 8.5 million gallons of crude oil. The oil formed a slick covering more than 1,400 sq. mi. (3,600 sq. km) and about 1,100 mi. (1,700 km) of shoreline was badly polluted.

Advancing sand dune

Sand storm

Wind breaks

Urbanization

▲ As the deserts spread, many people are forced to leave their homes and try to make a living elsewhere. Settlements grow larger, increasing pressure on the land.

▲ Dry sand and light soil can be held in place by nets or by spraying a protective film over it, to stop the processes of erosion.

▶ Nuclear waste remains dangerous for several centuries. It must be stored deep underground.

WASTE DISPOSAL
We produce millions of tons of waste every year from mines, factories, and homes. Most of the waste is buried in landfill sites. Although new sites are strictly controlled to ensure they are safe, toxic chemicals have leached from some old sites, contaminating the land and water supplies.

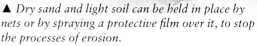

◀ The base of a landfill site is lined to prevent dirty liquids from leaking into nearby water. At the end of each day, the rubbish is leveled and covered with topsoil.

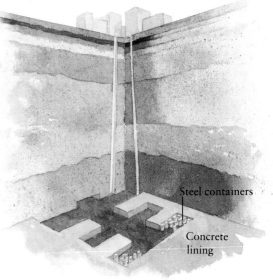

Steel containers

Concrete lining

Pollutants leach into water table

Conservation

Over the last 30 years, we have become aware of the damage we do to the environment. People have begun to find ways to reduce the amount of waste released into the air and water, and strict laws are applied by many governments. Ecologists and conservationists have found ways to help wildlife. Recycling has encouraged new uses for things that we used to throw away as garbage. Many problems remain, but progress has been made, and there have been many important improvements.

RECYCLED PAPER

About half of our domestic waste is paper which could be recycled. Recycling paper causes less pollution and protects the natural habitats cleared to plant the softwoods used to make new paper.

Symbol for recycled paper

GLASS AND ALUMINUM RECYCLING

Processing raw materials uses energy and causes pollution. Recycling often saves energy and resources, and reduces domestic waste as well as pollution. Old glass jars and bottles can be crushed and melted to make new glass objects. Extracting aluminum from its ore uses a great deal of energy, so recycling aluminum cans saves energy. It used to be expensive to recycle the cans, because they contained steel which had to be separated from the aluminum. Cans are now made from aluminum only.

Empty bottles

Recycling center

Glass is crushed and melted

Recycled glass

◀ Many towns now have recycling points, with containers for different items. Separating glass bottles into different colors makes the process easier. Some plastic bottles can also be recycled.

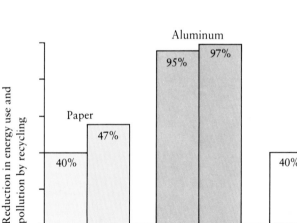

Reduction in energy use and pollution by recycling

Paper — Energy 40%, Pollution 47%
Aluminum — Energy 95%, Pollution 97%
Glass — Energy 40%, Pollution 45%

Energy   Pollution   Energy   Pollution   Energy   Pollution

Inner buffer zone

Core area

BIOSPHERE RESERVES

"Biosphere reserves" are a network of areas that will include examples of all the world's major types of vegetation. The reserves contain undisturbed vegetation and farmland and are managed for conservation. About 60 have been set up so far by the United Nations.

LANDSCAPE PRESERVATION

Attempts are now being made to reclaim land that has been used for mining or industry. Open-pit mines can be flooded, and turned into lakes for watersports and wildlife. Old industrial sites and garbage dumps tips can be covered with a thick layer of soil and turned into recreational land.

Old industrial site

CONSERVING HABITATS

International agreements exist to protect endangered species and to preserve their habitats. The habitats of migratory water birds are protected by the Ramsar Convention on Wetlands of International Importance. Other places are recognized by the United Nations as World Heritage Sites.

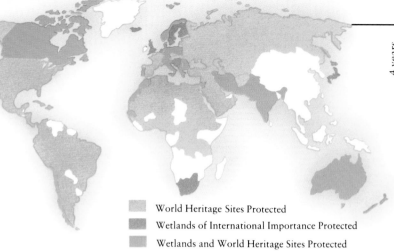

World Heritage Sites Protected

Wetlands of International Importance Protected

Wetlands and World Heritage Sites Protected

COUNTRIES WITH AGREEMENTS TO PROTECT WORLD HERITAGE SITES AND WETLANDS OF INTERNATIONAL IMPORTANCE

4 years

1 year

Outer buffer zone

▲ *The reserve has a protected core, and an inner "buffer" zone for research. Local people live in an outer buffer zone, which tourists are allowed to visit.*

BIOLOGICAL CONTROL

Pesticides are expensive and can cause pollution. "Biological control" uses natural enemies to control pests and weeds. For example, geese eat the weeds in fruit orchards, at the same time fertilizing the ground. Ladybugs are used to control aphids. Ducks are used by farmers in China to eat the insects that damage crops.

THE EARTH SUMMIT

In June 1992, the UN Conference on Environment and Development (the "Earth Summit") took place in Rio de Janeiro. Agreements were signed by many countries to limit climate change, and to protect species and habitats ("biodiversity"), sustainable development, and forest management. A program to achieve these aims was outlined.

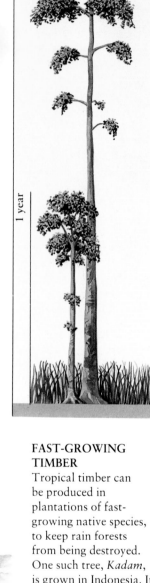

FAST-GROWING TIMBER

Tropical timber can be produced in plantations of fast-growing native species, to keep rain forests from being destroyed. One such tree, *Kadam*, is grown in Indonesia. It reaches 10 ft. (3 m) in its first year, then adds 6–10 ft. (2–3 m) a year for up to 8 years. Another Asian species, *Erima*, can grow to 80 ft. (25 m) in 4 years and 160 ft. (50 m) in 60 years.

Reclaimed land

◄ *Industrial wasteland can become a park with lakes and trees or playing fields.*

GLOSSARY

Words in **bold** indicate an entry elsewhere in the glossary.

Abrasion: Process of **erosion** in which particles of rock are worn away, and wear away a surface by being dragged over it or thrown against it.

Abyssal plain: Flat area of the ocean where depths exceed 6,600 ft. (2,000 m). Oozes (mud and other sediments) are deposited on the abyssal plain.

Active margin: Margin of a continent that is also a **plate** margin; it is associated with earthquake and volcanic activity and ocean trenches.

Agglomerate: **Igneous rock** made up of sharp fragments of different sizes. These may result from a volcanic explosion.

Alluvium: Sediment transported by a river or stream and deposited in its floodplain.

Amber: Fossilized sap of conifers. It hardens to a clear, brownish resin and may contain trapped insects.

Amethyst: Purple form of **quartz**.

Ammonites: Extinct **invertebrate** group related to squid and octopuses. The fossilized shell resembles a ridged pin-wheel. Ammonites are found in rocks from the Devonian to the Upper Cretaceous ages.

Andesite: Fine-grained volcanic rock.

Anthracite: Hard, jet-black form of **coal** which has a high carbon content.

Anticline: Arch-shaped **fold** in rocks with the oldest rocks in the core.

Anticyclone: Area of high **atmospheric pressure.**

Antiform: An arch-shaped **fold** in the rocks where the oldest rocks may not be in the center.

Aquifer: Mass of rock that is **permeable** to water and in which a large quantity of water may be stored.

Archipelago: Group of islands.

Artesian well: Well from which water flows without being pumped, because the head of the water in the **aquifer** lies above the level of the well head.

Asthenosphere: Weak zone in the upper **mantle** of the Earth which lies beneath the **lithosphere**.

Atmosphere: Layer of air that surrounds the Earth. The atmosphere is about 310 mi. (500 km) thick.

Atmospheric pressure: Downward force exerted by the weight of the air; 1,013 millibars at sea level.

Atoll: Ring-shaped coral **reef** that surrounds a lagoon. It often forms on a submerging **volcano**.

Aurora: Phenomenon of bright lights in the **atmosphere** caused by the **solar wind** entering the **ionosphere**.

Avalanche: Sudden rapid fall of rock or snow.

Badlands: Area of barren country where occasional heavy rainfall and little plant cover lead to severe **erosion**.

Barometer: Instrument for measuring **atmospheric pressure.**

Barrier reef: Coral **reef** that runs roughly parallel to a shoreline and is separated from the land by a **lagoon**.

Basalt: Blackish, fine-grained **igneous rock** formed from the hardened **lava** from a volcanic **eruption**.

Basin: Large depression in the Earth's **crust**.

Batholith: Large igneous **intrusion** that occurs at great depths.

Beaufort Scale: Scale of whole numbers from 0 to 12 used to describe wind strength.

Bedding: Sheetlike layers in which **sedimentary rocks** are deposited.

Belemnites: Extinct **invertebrate** group related to squid and octopuses. They had hard internal parts which, when found as fossils, resemble bullets. Belemnites are found in rocks from the Jurassic to the Upper Cretaceous.

Biosphere: Part of the Earth in which life is found.

Black smoker: Fissure in the seabed through which hot fluids flow into the sea water and mix with it to produce black, smokelike plumes.

Brachiopod: Also known as lampshell. Marine **invertebrate** with the body contained in a pair of hinged shells.

Breaker: Sea wave that is collapsing as it approaches the shore.

Breccia: Coarse-grained **sedimentary rock** made up of angular fragments of rock held together by some kind of mineral **cement**.

Calcite: Common rock-forming mineral (calcium carbonate). It is the main mineral in **limestone**.

Carbon cycle: Movement of the element carbon (C) through the interior, surface, and **atmosphere** of the Earth.

Caldera: Large, circular depression in the Earth's crust formed when the roof over a large mass of molten **igneous rock** collapses.

Cast: Replica of a **fossil** formed when the fossil itself is dissolved away and leaves a **mold**, which is then filled in by sediment.

Cement: Material such as **calcite** that passes into the spaces between sediments and then crystallizes out of solution to bind the sediment together.

Chalcopyrite: Common ore of copper. Because of its brassy yellow color and metallic **luster**, it is sometimes confused with gold. It is one of the minerals known as "fool's gold."

Chalk: Porous, fine-grained **sedimentary rock** that is hard when dry, and soft and claylike when saturated with water. It is composed of the **calcite** skeletons of tiny sea creatures called coccolithophores and foraminiferids.

Chert: Form of **silica** which lacks a **crystal** structure.

Cirque: Armchair-shaped depression in a mountainous region; it is formed by the scouring action of a **glacier**. Also known as a corrie (Scotland) or cwm (Wales).

Cirrus: Type of cloud seen as wispy streaks high in the sky.

Clay: **Sedimentary rock** in which the particles are less than 4 microns in diameter.

Cleavage: The way a **crystal** splits along a plane of weakness caused by the mineral's atomic structure.

Clint: Block of hard, horizontally bedded **limestone** which is isolated from its neighbors by **joints** known as **grikes**.

Coal: Rocklike deposit, rich in carbon and used as a fuel. It is formed from the remains of fossil plants.

Composite volcano: **Volcano** in which the cone is built up of alternating layers of **lava** and **ash**.

Conglomerate: Coarse-grained **sedimentary rock** made up of rounded fragments.

Constructive margin: Boundary zone between two **crustal plates** where new crust is being formed. The mid-Atlantic ridge is a constructive margin.

Contact metamorphism: Type of **metamorphism** caused by heat resulting from contact with a large body of **magma**.

Continental crust: Crust that lies underneath the continents. It is composed mainly of **granite**.

Continental drift: Idea put forward in 1910 that, throughout geological time, the Earth's continents have been moving in relation to one another.

Continental margin: Zone between the shoreline and the deep ocean floor. It includes the **continental shelf**, the **continental slope**, and the **continental rise**.

Continental rise: Ridge of sediment that forms at the bottom of the **continental slope**.

Continental shelf: Gently sloping zone between the shoreline and the top of the **continental slope**; it usually begins at a depth of about 500 ft. (150 m).

Continental slope: Steeply sloping zone between the bottom of the **continental shelf** and the beginning of the **continental rise**. It is usually cut by **submarine canyons** through which sediment from the land passes.

Convection current: Current within a fluid caused by temperature changes. Hot fluids are less dense than cool fluids and tend to rise. They then cool and fall again, causing a continuous current. Convection currents within the **asthenosphere** may lead to the processes of **plate tectonics**.

Core: Center of the Earth; it is divided into a solid inner core and a liquid outer core. The core is made mostly of nickel and iron at high pressures and temperatures.

Corrie: *see cirque*

Corundum: Hard mineral; sapphire and ruby are gem-quality forms of corundum.

Creep: Slow downhill movement of soil and subsoil caused by gravity.

Crust: Earth's outermost layer. It varies in thickness between about 3 mi. (5 km) under some parts of the ocean and 30 mi. (50 km) under mountain ranges.

Crystal: Solid body with a characteristic atomic structure, a definite chemical composition, regularly arranged plane faces, and a shape that reflects the internal structure.

Cuesta: Landform that resembles a long, low ridge with a steep slope on one side (the **scarp**) and a gentler slope on the other (the **dip** slope).

Cumulonimbus: Large cloud that towers up in a series of billowing cells, or smaller clouds, until it eventually flattens out to form an anvil shape. This is a typical rain cloud.

Cumulus: Bulging, dome-shaped cloud with a flat base; it resembles a cauliflower.

Cwm: *see cirque*

Cyclone: Region of low **atmospheric pressure**. Also called a depression.

Deep-sea trench: Deep, steep-sided trench more than 1,000 ft. (300 m) deeper than the neighboring ocean floor. Deep-sea trenches usually form at **destructive plate margins**.

Delta: Accumulation of sediments at the mouth of a river that resembles the shape of the Greek letter delta (Δ).

Depression: *see cyclone.*

Desert: Region in which the annual rainfall is less than 10 in. (250 mm). Deserts may be either hot or cold.

Desertification: Spread of desert conditions, often as a result of human interference, for example by cutting down large areas of forest.

Destructive margin: Boundary between two crustal **plates** that are moving toward one another, where one plate is diving beneath the other and destroying **oceanic crust**. **Earthquakes** and volcanic activity occur at destructive margins.

Diamond: Crystalline form of carbon; the hardest naturally occurring material.

Dike: Wall-like **intrusion** of **igneous rock** which cuts through the bedding of the surrounding rocks.

Dip: Angle formed between **beds** of rock and the horizontal.

Doldrums: Region close to the equator where winds are light.

Dolerite: Dark-colored, medium-grained **igneous rock** commonly found in **dikes**.

Dolomite: **Sedimentary rock** consisting of the rock-forming mineral also called dolomite.

Drainage pattern: Arrangement of the rivers and streams in an area. It is usually related to the geology of the area as well as its age.

Drift: Sediment deposited by a **glacier**.

Drumlin: Smooth, rounded, oval-shaped mound that is tapered at one end and blunt at the other. It may be made of glacial **drift** or of solid rock and is found in glaciated valleys.

Dry valley: Landform that resembles a river valley but contains no permanent stream.

Dune: Accumulation of windblown sand.

Earthquake: Movement within the Earth's **crust** that sends out shock waves when brittle rocks suddenly fracture.

El Niño: Current of warm water which, from time to time, flows southward along the coast of Ecuador and affects the climate throughout the Pacific.

Epicenter: Point on the Earth's surface immediately above the **hypocenter** of an **earthquake**.

Erosion: Wearing down of rocks and land surfaces through the movement of soil and rock debris by running water, wind, ice, and gravity.

Erratic: Boulder that has not come from the local rocks but has been transported to its present position by moving ice.

Eruption: Outpouring of gas, **lava**, ash, and other material from within the Earth, from a volcano or other opening, onto the surface, into the sea, or into the **atmosphere**.

Esker: Long, snakelike ridge of **drift** which has been laid down by the meltwater from a **glacier**.

Extinction: Complete death and therefore disappearance of a whole species of animals or plants.

Extrusion: Eruption of **magma** from a vent in the Earth's **crust**. A **volcano** is an extrusion.

Fault: Fracture or break in a body of rock that is too brittle to **fold**.

Feldspar: Important group of rock-forming minerals which includes orthoclase and plagioclase.

Fetch: Length of a stretch of water over which the wind is blowing to generate waves. The longer the fetch, the bigger the waves will be.

Fjord: (also fiord) Deep, narrow, U-shaped coastal inlet formed from a drowned glacial valley.

Flint: Variety of **chert** which often occurs as knobbly lumps in **chalk**.

Fog: Condition in which the air near the Earth's surface is almost saturated. The air contains suspended droplets of water that obscure vision.

Fold: Bend in the beds of rock.

Fossil: Remains or trace of an animal or plant preserved in the rocks. It is usually more than 10,000 years old.

Fracture: Clean break in a rock or mineral that is not caused by **cleavage** and is not related to the atomic structure of the mineral.

Front: Boundary between two different air masses.

Fumarole: Volcanic vent through which steam and gas are emitted.

Gabbro: Dark, coarse-grained **igneous rock** formed deep within the Earth.

Gaia hypothesis: Theory, developed by James Lovelock, suggesting that once life has begun on a planet, living things modify the conditions on the planet so that life is likely to be maintained.

Geological timescale: System that divides into named units all time since the Earth was formed.

Geyser: Vent in the Earth's crust that spouts a fountain of boiling water at intervals.

Glaciation: Covering of a large area of land by ice; an **ice age**.

Glacier: Large mass of moving ice. The effects of a glacier on, for example, a river valley can be easily recognized once the ice has retreated.

Gondwanaland: Supercontinent that existed in the Southern Hemisphere before continental drifting divided it into South America, Africa, India, Australia, New Zealand, and Antarctica.

Graben: Troughlike structure which results from the downward movement of a block of **crust** between two almost vertical **fault** lines.

Granite: Coarse-grained, pale-colored **igneous rock** consisting mainly of the minerals **quartz, feldspar, and mica.**

Graptolites: Extinct group of sea-dwelling animals that lived in small colonies. Each individual was contained in a tube-like structure. Some colonies resemble tuning forks in shape. Graptolites lived between the Middle Cambrian and Lower Carboniferous Periods.

Greenhouse effect: Process in which the lower **atmosphere** is warmed. Clouds and gases such as carbon dioxide absorb and reradiate the sunlight reflected from the Earth's surface.

Grike: Widened **joint** separating one **clint** from another.

Guyot: Flat-topped, undersea mountain.

Gyre: Circular or spiral current of water.

Hail: Irregular pellets or rounded balls of ice that fall from the clouds like frozen rain.

Hanging valley: Valley formed by a **tributary** stream to a main valley that has been deepened by a **glacier**. The floor of the hanging valley is much higher than that of the main valley, and the tributary may flow into the larger river via a waterfall.

Hawaiian eruption: Volcanic **eruption** in which the basalt lavas are very fluid and where there are often fire fountains. Volcanic cones formed by Hawaiian eruptions have gently sloping sides.

Hematite: Important iron **ore**.

Hog's back: Landscape feature; a long narrow ridge formed where the **bedding** of the underlying rocks **dips** at an angle of 40° or more.

Hornblende: Important rock-forming mineral.

Horst: Block of rock thrust upward between two nearly vertical **faults**.

Hot spot: Area of volcanic activity that is more or less stationary. It may form where there is a rising **convection current** in the **mantle**.

Humus: Decayed remains of plant material found in soil.

Hurricane: Violent tropical storm which occurs in the Caribbean area and on the northeastern coast of Australia. It is caused by a deep **cyclone**.

Hydrological cycle: Water cycle; the flow of water through the **atmosphere**, land, oceans, seas, rivers, lakes, and living things.

Hydrosphere: All of the water that occurs at the Earth's surface.

Hygrometer: Instrument for measuring humidity—the amount of moisture in the **atmosphere**.

Hypocenter: Center or focus of an **earthquake**.

Ice age: Period during the Earth's history when the polar ice caps have expanded to cover large parts of other continents. There is also a fall in the average global temperature.

Igneous rock: Rock, such as **granite** or **basalt**, that has formed by crystallization from a hot **magma**.

Impermeable: Describes rocks that water or other liquids cannot pass through.

Impervious: Describes rocks that do not allow water, oil, or gas to flow through them.

Inorganic: Substances that do not have a living origin, for example, minerals.

Intrusion: Body of **igneous rock**, such as a **batholith**, that has been thrust into existing or "country" rocks.

Invertebrate: Animal that lacks a backbone. The great majority of the Earth's animals are invertebrates.

Ionosphere: Part of the Earth's **atmosphere**, above a height of about 50 mi. (80 km), where there are more free charged particles (ions and electrons).

Island arc: Group of volcanic islands situated close to a **deep-sea trench** where one crustal **plate** is being pulled beneath another.

Isobar: Line on a weather map that links points of equal **atmospheric pressure**.

Jet stream: High-speed flow of air that travels for great distances at heights of between 7 and 8 mi. (11 and 13 km).

Joint: Break in a rock where there has been little movement along the line of the joint.

Karst: Area of **limestone** country with characteristics such as cavern systems, **sinkholes**, and limestone **pavements**.

Kettle hole: Depression, sometimes filled with water, in an area of glacial **drift**. It is formed by melting ice.

Laccolith: Igneous **intrusion**, shaped like a lens, with a domed roof and flat base, which has been thrust between the layers of other rocks.

Lagoon: Area of shallow water at the coast on the landward side of a reef or group of islands.

Laurasia: Supercontinent that existed in the Northern Hemisphere before **continental drifting** separated it into North America, Europe, and Asia.

Lava: Hot, molten rock erupted from a **volcano**.

Limestone: Sedimentary rock made up mainly of **calcite** or **dolomite**.

Lithosphere: Upper, rocky layer of the Earth which includes the **crust** and the upper region of the **mantle**.

Longshore drift: Drifting of sand and pebbles along a beach. Longshore drift results from sea currents caused by **prevailing winds**.

Lopolith: Saucer-shaped igneous **intrusion** thrust between the layers of surrounding rock.

Luster: Describes the way **minerals** reflect light.

Magma: Body of molten rock.

Magnetic poles: Two points on the Earth's surface (north and south) to which a compass needle points. At the poles themselves a magnetized needle will point vertically downward.

Magnetite: Magnetic **ore** of iron, also known as lodestone.

Mantle: Layer of the Earth lying between the **core** and the **crust**. It is hot and the lower part is thought to be in a semi-**plastic** state.

Marble: **Metamorphic rock** that is formed when **limestone** or **dolomite** are subjected to heat and/or pressure.

Meander: Turn or winding of a stream or river.

Meltwater: Water that has melted from a **glacier** or other body of ice.

Mercalli scale: Scale, from 1 to 12, for measuring the intensity of an **earthquake** based on its observed effects.

Mesa: Flat-topped hill formed by river action on horizontal beds of rock.

Mesosphere: Part of the Earth's **atmosphere**, between about 30 and 50 mi. (50–80 km) in height.

Metamorphic rock: Rock that has been formed by the effects of heat and/or pressure on an existing rock so that the minerals have **recrystallized**—a changed rock.

Metamorphism: Process by which a rock changes through heat and/or pressure.

Meteorite: Small body of rocky or metallic material that enters the Earth's **atmosphere** from space and hits the ground.

Micas: Rock-forming minerals with a sheetlike structure found in many **metamorphic** and **igneous rocks**.

Mid-ocean ridge: Long ridge of active **volcanoes** in the middle of the ocean floor, where new **crust** is being created, and two **plates** are being forced apart through **seafloor spreading**. The mid-Atlantic ridge is an example.

Mineral: Naturally occurring substance with a crystalline structure and definite chemical composition. Rocks are composed of minerals.

Mohorovičić discontinuity: Boundary between the **crust** and **mantle**, defined by the effects on **earthquake** waves.

Mohs' scale of hardness: Scale devised by the German scientist Friedrich Mohs (1773–1839) to estimate the hardness of **minerals** by their ability to scratch a set of standard minerals. Talc is very soft and is the mineral used to define 1 on the scale. It can be scratched by gypsum and other minerals of hardness 2. The other minerals in the series are calcite 3; fluorite 4; apatite 5; orthoclase 6; quartz 7; topaz 8; corundum 9; diamond 10.

Monsoon: Seasonal change in the **prevailing wind** direction which may bring a dramatic change in weather, such as the rainy season in India.

Moraine: Ridge of **drift** left behind by a melting **glacier**.

Native element: Element, such as gold, which occurs in its pure form in the Earth's crust.

Oasis: Area in a desert where a regular supply of water, often from an underground source, enables a lush vegetation to thrive in fertile soils.

Oceanic crust: Rocks beneath the ocean bed and above the **Mohorovičić discontinuity**. Oceanic crust is composed mainly of **basalt**.

Olivine: Important rock-forming mineral found in **basalts** and **gabbros**.

Oolite: Type of **limestone** made up of rounded particles of calcium carbonate called ooliths.

Ore mineral: Mineral from which economically important amounts of a metal can be obtained.

Organic: Anything that has a living origin, for example, plants, animals, and their remains.

Outcrop: Rock exposed at the Earth's surface.

Ozone layer: Layer in the **atmosphere** at a height of 10–20 mi. (15–30 km) where the form of oxygen called ozone (O_3) occurs in higher concentrations than usual. Ultraviolet (UV) light from the Sun is absorbed by ozone, converting it into the normal form of oxygen (O_2). This process reduces the amount of potentially harmful UV radiation that reaches the Earth's surface.

Pack ice: Area in the seas of polar regions where large blocks of ice are tightly packed together and move with the winds or currents.

Paleontology: Science in which fossils are studied.

Pangaea: Single supercontinent from which all the current continents evolved by splitting up and slowly drifting apart.

Passive margin: Margin of a continent that is not the margin of a crustal **plate**.

Pavement: Area of bare, relatively flat rock resembling a road.

Peat: Black soil type with little or no structure, formed by the breakdown of plant material in wet, airless conditions.

Pegmatite: Very coarse-grained **igneous rock**.

Peléan eruption: Violent volcanic **eruption** where the **lavas** are very thick and clouds of gas-charged material are emitted.

Peridotite: Coarse-grained **igneous rock** rich in **olivine**. Much of the **mantle** is composed of this rock.

Permafrost: Permanently frozen ground.

Permeable: Describing rock through which water or other liquids can seep.

Petroleum: Naturally occurring crude oil.

Petrology: Scientific study of rocks.

Phaccolith: Igneous **intrusion** that follows the **folds** of rock layers.

Phyllite: Fine-grained **metamorphic rock** formed from **mudstones** and **shales**; it has a layered structure and silky sheen.

Pillow lava: Formation of **lava** that resembles a pile of pillows, caused by the lava erupting underwater.

Pitchstone: Solidified glassy **lava** with a waxy appearance.

Plastic: Describes rock material in the **asthenosphere**, which, because of the temperature and pressure, can be deformed very slowly.

Plate: Major portion of the **lithosphere** with little volcanic or earthquake activity; it is bounded by **active margins** with other **plates**. The movement of the Earth's crustal plates in relation to one another causes **continental drift**.

Plate tectonics: Single model of how the outer part of the Earth works; it explains **continental drift, seafloor spreading,** and volcanic and earthquake activity.

Polar reversal: Reversal of the Earth's **magnetic poles**. It occurs about every 20–50 million years.

Precipitation: All forms in which water falls from the **atmosphere** to the ground; including rain, **sleet, hail,** and snow.

Prevailing wind: Commonest wind direction over a period of time in a given area.

Pumice: Volcanic rock that has been so strongly charged with gas that it has a frothy appearance and floats on water.

Pyrite: Yellow mineral also called iron pyrites or fool's gold.

Pyroxene: Important group of rock-forming minerals, such as augite.

Quartz: Silica, the important rock-forming mineral used to make glass.

Quartzite: Metamorphic rock composed mainly of quartz and formed from the metamorphism of quartz sandstones.

Rainbow: Arc-shaped spectrum of colors that forms in the sky when sunlight is split up by moisture in the atmosphere.

Raised beach: Beach from an earlier period that is now above the level of the shoreline, either because the sea level has fallen or the land has risen.

Recrystallization: Growth of new crystals in a rock as a result of the effects of heat and/or pressure.

Reef: Narrow, wall-like ridge of rock, usually limestone, that builds up in the sea as a result of the activity of animals such as corals.

Richter scale: Scale (from 1 to 10) that measures the intensity of earthquakes, based on the size of the shock waves.

Regional metamorphism: Type of metamorphism that occurs where plates are moving together.

Rift valley: Major trough in the Earth's crust bounded by faults.

Roche moutonné: Hump-shaped rock that has been smoothed on one side by a moving glacier and is rough and shattered on the opposite side.

Rock: Mass of minerals which may or may not be cemented together.

Salinity: Measure of the solids, including common salt, dissolved in the sea in parts per thousand. The salinity of sea water is about 35 parts per thousand.

Salt lake: Lake with a salinity of about 100 parts per thousand or more.

Sandstone: Sedimentary rock made up of grains of sand cemented together.

Savanna: Area on the edge of the tropics where rainfall is seasonal; typically, it is a region of coarse grassland with scattered trees.

Scarp: Steep slope or cliff associated with an almost flat tract of land. It results from the erosion of horizontal or gently sloping rocks by a river valley. Also called escarpment.

Schist: Medium-grained metamorphic rock with a layered structure and a sheen caused by mica minerals. Schists result from regional metamorphism.

Scree: Broken and shattered pieces of rock that accumulate down the slope of a rock face. It is caused by weathering and erosion of the rock.

Seafloor spreading: Process by which new oceanic crust is created at plate margins marked by mid-ocean ridges.

Sedimentary rock: Type of rock, such as sandstone or limestone, formed from the accumulation and hardening of fragments of other rocks, organic material, or minerals deposited from solution.

Seismic wave: Shock wave from an earthquake.

Seismology: Study of seismic waves from an earthquake.

Seismometer: Instrument used to detect seismic waves.

Shale: Fine-grained sedimentary rock with a sheetlike (platy) structure.

Silica: Silicon dioxide, which commonly occurs as quartz.

Sill: Shelflike body of igneous rock that has been thrust between the bedding of the country rocks.

Sinkhole: Steep-sided depression in a limestone area, formed by acid water dissolving away the limestone where two vertical joints have crossed.

Slate: Fine-grained metamorphic rock with a leafy or sheetlike structure.

Sleet: Mixture of falling rain and melting snow.

Smog: Mixture of smoke and fog.

Solar wind: Stream of protons, electrons, and other high-energy particles that stream from the Sun.

Spit: Arm of sand and/or gravel that juts out into the sea from the shore.

Stack: Pillar of rock formed by the erosion of an arch that has been worn out of a cliff by the sea.

Stalactite: Column of limestone hanging from the roof of a cavern where there is a constant dripping of lime-rich water. It is formed as calcium carbonate comes out of solution.

Stalagmite: Column of limestone standing up from the floor of a cavern where lime-rich water drips.

Steppe: Vast, usually treeless plain where temperatures vary greatly between night and day, winter and summer.

Stratocumulus: Type of cloud consisting of flat, grayish white layers.

Stratosphere: Layer of the atmosphere between about 6–30 mi. (10–50 km).

Streak: Color of a mineral in its fresh, powdered form.

Strombolean eruption: Volcanic eruption in which there are frequent, medium-sized eruptions and small explosions.

Submarine canyon: Deep valley that cuts through the continental shelf.

Syenite: Coarse-grained igneous rock.

Syncline: Trough-shaped fold with younger rocks in the center.

Synform: Trough-shaped fold in which younger rocks may not always be in the center.

Thermal: Rising air current caused by heating from below.

Tide: Rise and fall of the world's oceans, caused by the gravitational attraction mainly of the Moon but also the Sun.

Tornado: Twisting column of air where the wind speeds are very high.

Trade winds: Prevailing winds that blow in the tropics from about 30° north to 30° south. They blow from the northeast in the Northern Hemisphere and from the southeast in the Southern Hemisphere.

Transpiration: Process in which moisture is taken up from the soil through the roots of plants, moves up the stem, and evaporates through pores in the leaves.

Trilobite: Extinct sea creature related to insects, with a body divided longways into three sections. Trilobites lived from Cambrian to Permian times.

Troposphere: Layer of the atmosphere from the Earth's surface to a height of about 6 mi. (10 km), where weather occurs.

Tsunami: Large sea wave caused by an earthquake or volcanic explosion. It is often wrongly called a tidal wave.

Typhoon: Powerful cyclone that occurs in the western Pacific and China Sea.

Unconformity: Surface between two beds of rock, which represents a break in the deposition of sediments.

Vein: Mineral deposit in a rock fracture.

Vesuvian eruption: Volcanic eruption where explosions take place after long quiet periods.

Volcanic bomb: Lump of lava that is thrown out of a volcano and takes on a characteristic shape during its flight.

Volcano: Vent in the Earth's crust through which lava, gas, ash, and fragments of solid rock are ejected.

Weathering: Breakdown of rocks at the Earth's surface, for example, through heating and cooling, frost shattering, and dissolving by acid rainwater.

INDEX

Page numbers in *italic* type refer to the illustrations.
Page numbers in **bold** type refer to key topics.

A

Acid rain 79, *79*
Advection fog 57, *57*
Africa: continental drift 23; grasslands 68, 69, *69*; Great Rift Valley 29, *29*, *48*; plate tectonics 25, *25*, 29
Agriculture *63*, 73, 80, *80*
Air 51, *51*; *see also* Atmosphere
Air mass 53
Air pollution 17, **78–79**, *78–79*
Aklé dunes 71
Alaska 64, 65, *65*, 81, *81*
Alps 26, 27, *27*
Altocumulus clouds 56, 59
Altostratus clouds 56
Aluminum 15, 32, 76, 82
Amazon River 46
Amber *34*, 84
Ammonites *34–35*, 35, 84
Andes Mountains 26, 27, 40, 46
Anemometers 54, 60
Angel Falls 46
Animals: carbon cycle 17; continental drift 22; fossils **34–35**, *34–35*; grasslands 69; mountainous areas 27; ocean life 43, *43*; oxygen cycle 17; temperate woodland 66; tundra 64
Antarctic *16*, 23, 25, 39, 54, 64–65, *65*, 71, 78, 79
Antarctic Ocean 40
Anticline 29, 84
Antiform 29, 84
Appalachian Mountains 27, 66
Aquifers 71, *71*, 84
Arctic *16*, 53, 54, 57, 61, 64–65, *65*, 78
Arctic Ocean *40*
Argon 51
Aristotle 10
Asia 66, 68
Asthenosphere *14*, 22, 24, *24*, 84
Atlantic Ocean 22, 23, *23*, 40, *40*; hurricanes 55; plate tectonics 24, 25, *25*; Sargasso Sea 43
Atlas Mountains 27
Atmosphere: **50–51**, *50–51*, 84; balance **16–17**; climate 52; pollution **78–79**, *78–79*; radiation from Sun *13*, 17; water vapor 40
Atolls 41, *41*, 84
Augite 32, *32*
Aurorae *15*, *50*, 84
Australia 23, *23*, 25, 55, 66, 68, 69, *69*, *77*

B

Baker, H.B. 23
Balloons, weather 61
Barchan dunes 71, *71*
Barographs 60, *60*
Barometers 60, 84
Bars 45
Basalt *14*, 25, 30, *30*, 84
Bauxite 76, *76*
Baikal, Lake 48, *48*
Beaches 45, *45*
Beaufort wind scale 54, 84
Ben Nevis 36
Biological pest control 83
Biomes 62
Biosphere reserves 82, *83*
Birds 83
Bogs 49, *49*
Bornhardts 69
Britain 67, 77
Broadleaved trees 66–67, *67*

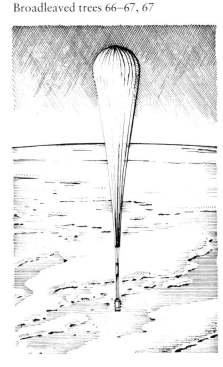

C

Calcium 15, 32
Caldera 20, 84
Calgary, Canada 59
California Current 53
Cambrian Period *30–31*
Canada 57, 64, 65, 66
Canadian Shield 27
Carbon *33*, 74
Carbon cycle 17, *17*, 84
Carbon dioxide 13, 16, 17, 36, 51, *51*, 78, 79
Carboniferous Period *30–31*

Carrara marble quarry *31*
Caspian Sea 48, *49*
Caves and caverns 37, *37*
Cenozoic Era *30–31*
Chalk 30, *30*, 84
Chaos theory 61
Cherrapunji, India 53, 59
Chicago 59
Chile 66
China 66
Chinook wind 54
Chlorine 78
Chlorofluorocarbons (CFCs) 78, 79
Cirques 39, 84
Cirrocumulus clouds 56
Cirrostratus clouds 55, 56
Cirrus clouds 53, 55, 56, 84
Clay 30, 84
Cliffs 44, 45
Climate 13, 44, 51, **52–53**, *52–53*, 62, 79, *79*
Clouds 10, 50, 51, 55, **56–57**, *56–57*, *58–59*, 61
Coal 34, *34*, 65, 74, *74*, 75, 84
Coasts 44–45, *44–45*
Colombia 73
Color: rainbows 59, *59*; skies 60, *60*
Compasses 15, *15*
Coniferous forests 66–67, *66*
Conservation 82–83, *82–83*
Continental drift 22–23, *22–23*, 24, 85
Continental plates 22, *22*, 25
Continental shelf 40, 85
Copper 76, *76*, 77
Coral reefs 41, *41*
Core, Earth's 15, 85
Coriolis effect 53, *53*, 54
Corries 85
Cretaceous Period *30–31*
Crust, Earth's 14, *14*, 15, 25, *25*, 26, 85
Crystals 32, *33*, 58, *58*, 85
Cumulonimbus clouds 55, 56, 85
Cumulus clouds 56, 57, 85
Currents, ocean 42, *42*, 43, 53
Cwms 85
Cyclones 55, 85

D

Dams 48, 75
Dating rocks 35
Days 12
Dead Sea 32, 42
Death Valley 71
Deciduous forests 66–67, *66*
Deforestation 17, *67*, 73, 80, *80*

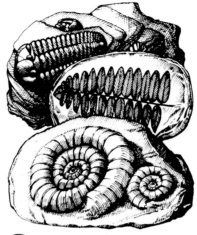

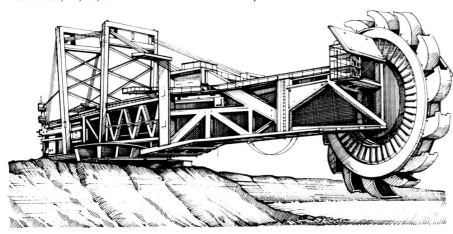

The publishers would like to thank the following artists
for contributing to the book:

Kevin Addison 15
Richard Bonson 13, 16–17, 25, 30–31, 36, 46–47
Lynn Chadwick (Garden Studio) 44–45
Dean Entwistle 19, 20–21, 25
Chris Forsey 20–21, 23, 24, 38–39
Mark Franklin 33, 67
Ray Grinaway 49, 62, 64
André Hrydziusko (Simon Girling Associates) 60–61
Roger Kent (Garden Studio) 47, 48, 62–63, 68–69, 72–73
Adrian Lascom (Garden Studio) 49
Jenny Lloyd (The Classroom) 11, 13, 16, 23, 24, 22–23, 35, 58, 76
Maltings Partnership 18–19, 20–21, 22–23, 22, 24–25, 32–33, 37, 38, 40–41, 42–43, 45,
46–47, 48–49, 53, 56–57, 58–59, 64, 66–67, 68, 70, 72, 74–75, 76–77, 78–79, 80–81, 82–83
Josephine Martin (Garden Studio) 32–33, 34–35, 70–71
Doreen McGuinness (Garden Studio) 10–11, 19
David More (Linden Artists) 66–67
Oxford Illustrators 53, 78, 81
Nick Shewring (Garden Studio) 15, 42, 65, 83
Roger Stewart 10–11, 12–13, 14–15, 22–23, 40–41, 43, 50–51, 63, 65, 66, 68, 70, 72, 74
Steve Weston 50
Keith Woodcock 61

The publishers wish to thank the following for supplying
photographs for this book:

Page 8 ZEFA; 15 NASA; 22 ZEFA; 28 ZEFA; 29 Ardea; 31 AGE Fotostock; 32 ZEFA; 36 ZEFA;
42 Science Photo Library; 46 Frank Spooner; 51 NASA; 52 Science Photo Library; 55 Frank Spooner
Pictures; 57 ZEFA; 61 Dundee University; 67 ZEFA; 69 Frank Spooner; 73 ZEFA; 75 Spectrum;
81 ZEFA